THE REPTILIAN GODDESS
AND MILLION COPS

PREMKUMAR

notionpress.com

INDIA · SINGAPORE · MALAYSIA

ISBN
Paperback 979-8-89777-363-3
Hardcase 979-8-89906-304-6

Table of Contents

Foreword

The author migrated to Hyderabad in search of livelihood and found a job as a junior functionary in a public sector undertaking He was struggling to raise a child and found himself and his child in a center of a hate crime. One migrant worker from coastal Andhra took instant hatred towards his family and unknown him at that time that worker was also a master of witch craft.

That worker was stealing his earnings without his knowledge and so he was always running short of money. After practicing his trade for many years, that worker thought of a final solution by involving a honey trap. Fortunately despite many efforts of that person, there was a Sufi saint in his life who protected the author and his family. As he was made a subject of intense surveillance, the author thought of a nickname for himself, that is Johnny Relevant.

Back in his college days, when porn was limited to color photos and books, the author was stuck by one character by name Johnny Relevant by an unknown author. That Johnny was all things to all people; if they were looking for a blonde, tall blue eyed Adonis, our JR transforms himself to fit that role. Or if they were looking for a doddering old man with watery eyes, our Johnny transforms himself into that role looking guilty as hell.

So when the cops were looking for someone who robbed a bank, derailed a train or blew up a landmine, he became an automatic suspect basking in their rich attention. But they never realized that there is a divine feminine power which shielded him and his family from unjust actions of law enforcement agencies. This book is a testament to her power and glory.

Huligamma Devi Our Ancestral Goddess

A tribute to her power and glory

Long ago, two devotees of Renuka Devi consort of Sage Jamadagni and mother of Lord Parashurama used to live in a small village called Huligi on the banks of river Tungabhadra in Karnataka state in India. The river was the border between British India and kingdom of Nizam of Hyderabad.

A dam was constructed between two hillocks by Thirumalay Iyengar on the river in 1950 impounding 100 tmc of water which made the nearby town of Hospet prosperous due to irrigation. It was a joint venture between Governments of Karnataka and Andhra Pradesh.

Any way before twentieth century, Tungabhadra River was a free flowing perennial river flooding the banks during the rainy seasons. The two devotees of Renuka Devi used to visit her temple at Saudatti village near Belgaum on every full moon. It was a rainy season, and the rain was in full fury. The brothers were unable to visit her temple at Saudatti and were much distressed. That night Devi appeared in their dream and consoled them. She told them not to be distressed due to their inability to visit Saudatti as she has taken her form as Srichakra in Huligi itself and showed them the location. On digging the land, they were overjoyed to find a Srichakra to the west of nearby Somashwera temple.

She was worshipped for the last eight centuries and devotees from the other side of the river used to visit the temple by crossing the river in round vessels made of bamboo. Later the British constructed a bridge on the river using granite and meter gauge trains were running between Guntakal and Hubli. The same bridge was upgraded to broad gauge during the nationwide unigauge conversion programme.

As the temple falls under the jurisdiction of Nizam state, it was attacked by Razakars during the Police action launched by Vallabhai Patel. The Nizam was resisting integration of his kingdom into Indian Union. To avoid that he unleashed a reign of terror using his militia called Razakars. The slaughtered innocents raped and plundered all Hindus. After Patel ordered police action, Indian army entered by trains from Bellary. The author's grandfather was the loco pilot ferrying the troops and causalities from the battle zone. Murdering innocents is one thing but fighting a battle hardened army is altogether different ball game. The war was over in just three days

They hunted down the Razakars and some of them after committing murder and mayhem were hiding under dead bodies in the temple premises. The goddess warned the priest of the temple about them who in turn alerted the army. The hiding Razakars were found, pulled out and shot dead by the army. Their graves might be seen even now by the side of the canal.

The author is the eldest son among five siblings and the family used to visit the temple whenever his father used to come on annual leave. The author was not a particularly bright in studies and was always forgetful. His elder cousins tried to teach him unsuccessfully and finally gave up claiming that he would not complete even matriculation. But right from childhood, he was attached to that temple and used to visit on Fridays.

After some years he used to feel some connection being made in his brain. He passed degree in science and later got an engineering degree also. Later the author got a job in HAL and became a victim of a hate crime. Powerful witchcraft was unleashed with a honey trap case was foisted bringing entire family under intense scrutiny. Just as the security apparatus about to whisk him away on suspicion of indulging in unlawful activities, the goddess sent a message through a Sufi saint to perform a simple pooja; that is donate home cooked food and a new cloth to any married female for 11 weeks. He followed it and was relieved from that job through a VRS scheme especially tailored to his service record.

So he got out of HAL safely and yet the security apparatus was suspicious of his actions. He left his job in HAL and after many years of unemployment found a job as a techno commercial manager for a Bangalore based defense procurement. His job would take him to all the defense undertaking around Hyderabad seeking orders for his company. All the while he was under intense scrutiny for some unknown reasons. As the security apparatus was about to pounce on him and his family, the goddess appeared as a huge reptile lifting him by his cap to an unknown location. Some months later he got a job in Odisha as a senior faculty away from the defense industry of Hyderabad. Unknown to him that place in Odisha was a hot bed of insurgency and so the apparatus tried to connect him to their cause unsuccessfully. Goddess promised him protection from them all the time so they could not do any harm.

One sees many transgenders clad in sarees singing praises to the goddess. Some of them were males who mocked the goddess or her rituals and found themselves emasculated. Whoever makes fun or ridicules her temple or her devotees become transgenders.

During the reign of Tipu sultan, the village of Huligi was subjected to invasion by the Mysore kingdom. The local chieftain was a ardent devotee of Huligamma Devi. The tiny principality was no match to the mighty army of Tipu sultan. So the local chieftain had no way of countering the mighty army of Tipu sultan. He cloistered himself in the sanctum sanctorum of the temple and beseeched the goddess to save his kingdom and people from the invaders.

One night a fierce whirlwind descended on the camp of Mysore army the horses were terrified. Their tents were blown away throwing the Mysore army into disarray. One lady in white appeared in the tempest and warned the attackers to retreat before great calamity befall them. Next day he attackers lifted the siege leaving the kingdom of Huligi in peace.

Coming to the present. The author ventured into Christianity to seek remedy from unemployment and homelessness. He met a highly gifted celibate young preacher from Mysore. He settled in a small village called Kadderampura on the way to the historical Hampi for his evangelical mission. One day he asked me join in his prayer session which I agreed with an open mind. He prayed with much fervor and passion and I felt earth shaking under my feet. Then he stopped suddenly and said" There is a blue green entity with fangs behind you and it is saying to you that all your prayers are waste. You will only hang yourself."

After listening to this, I became confused and wondered did Jesus not say "I am the way and truth. No one comes to the Father except through Me.? Needless to say that all the prophesies given by that young preacher failed to manifest as predicted.

I was thrown into utter confusion about universality of Christianity and its doctrine. There is no syncretism between Hinduism and Christianity notwithstanding the claims made by some pseudo spiritual gurus about the Oneness of all religions.

In another incident I must mention about a preacher by name Venkat Reddy aka Philip Reddy. He was a hard core naxalite and survived many encounters. He showed me the bullet holes in his legs as a legacy of his colorful and dangerous past. He killed in cold blood many opponents and was sentenced to death not once but three times only to be reprieved at the last minute. He was the really Chosen One as Jesus did many miracles in his life. He was instrumental in getting two convicts on death row reprieve and commuted to life sentence.

A short digression: Two unemployed youth wanted to become rich by holding up passengers of a bus to ransom. To that end they procured a plastic bottle filled with petrol and boarded an night express bus at a place called Chilakaluripeta. After the bus reached a desolate stretch of road away from municipal limits, they got up in the bus and brandished the bottle of petrol demanding the passengers to hand over their cash and gold. While the stunned passengers were getting ready to comply with their demand, one of them poured petrol from the bottle on to the floor to threaten the passengers. To further threaten the passengers, the other one lighted a match stick which started an inferno in the bus. That was totally unexpected by the potential robbers. As the inferno spread throughout the bus within seconds, nobody could escape from the bus. All the passengers were burnt to death in their seats with the driver remaining a mute spectator.

There was utter shock and confusion in Government as none knew anything about the perpetrators. It was not known whether the robbers were also burnt or survived. As their bodies could not be found, it was surmised that they have survived and made good their escape.

A biggest manhunt was launched and cops rounded up many potential suspects only to find them not involved in that crime. Hundreds of cops were pulled out to find some clue around that place called. Chilakaluripeta.

One cop in plain clothes was roaming in the town and came to a place where a building was being constructed. There he saw two guys bending rods for making pillars for concrete. To his cop's eye something seemed to be out of place. To further boost his suspicion he found them to be with shaved heads.

The cop stopped at the nearby tea stall and enquired about those two guys. He asked whether the two guys returned from Thirupathi where the devotees shave their heads to fulfill a vow. The hotel person said they were there previous day also and definitely not been to any temple recently.

To the keen eye of the cop the two guys were nervous about something and so he called back up. Reinforcements arrived and they were quickly whisked off to the police station.

Under interrogation it turned out the guys were the potential robbers whose get rich plan went horribly wrong burning thirty innocents persons in their seats. They were also badly burnt in that inferno with almost all their hair singed out. To hide it they got their heads shaved clean.

It was an open and shut case and they were given death sentence in the sessions court and upheld by the high court. The appeal in Supreme Court went against them as the court confirmed the death sentence.

Now enter our Venkat Reddy aka Phillip Reddy: He got an appeal drafted to submit to the then President Dr Shankar Dayal Sharma. He sought and got an appointment with the President of India and pleaded with him to commute the death sentence to one of life imprisonment. The President finally commuted their sentence to life sentence and the two convicts were moved to normal jail.

The author met that preacher by name Philip Reddy and visited his place several times. Once he visited the author's home for prayer and went away. The next day he came back with a strange account.

After praying and reaching his home, the preacher went to bed in the night as usual. In the night a female clad in white appeared and became a huge snake as big as a Anaconda. Then she wrapped around his body twisting him into contortions all the while screaming "How dare you to come to my home?"

The next day the world renowned preacher visited the author's place narrating that incident with the reptilian goddess. His body was paining with the treatment received from the Reptilian Goddess and he advised me to fast on Tuesdays and Fridays the days of worship of Huligamma Devi.

In the Old Testament of the Bible, Moses asks Israelites when bitten by poisonous snakes as punishment for their sins, to look up at the bronze snake held upon a pole for healing. Numbers 21; 8&9

But seven centuries later Hezekiah destroys all places of worship including the bronze snake Moses installed. The reasons are obscure. Also Jesus in the New Testament says" Just as Moses lifted up the snake in the wilderness, so the Son of Man must be lifted up,[a] 15 that everyone who believes may have eternal life in him."[b]

Glory to Huligamma Devi.

Tag words; Saudatti, Tungabhadra, Sri Chakra, Police action, Razakars, Naxalites. John 3:14-15, Numbers 21:8&9

The Reptilian Goddess and Million Cops

A tribute to the power and glory of Huligamma Devi of Munirabad on the banks of Tungabhadra River in Karnataka state

Johnny Relevant was getting ready for that day's rendezvous with the German principal. His MD is coming from Bangalore and the taxi was arranged to pick him from the hotel and the German principal is to be also picked up from his hotel and after breakfast, meeting is arranged with the scientists of DMRL. JR already submitted details of his passport and got the appointment at 11 AM at the lounge. Being foreigner, he can't be admitted beyond the lounge and there are ample arrangements for presentations if necessary in the lounge itself.

Prior to this job, JR was working as foreman in an engineering college with starvation wages. Since he didn't have a PG, he could not be given teaching assignments as per rules. But he was regularly attending prayer meeting at one preacher by name Sarah Naidu on every Sunday. She was a single mother who became a preacher for the sake of her children when her husband abandoned them.

In one such meeting, the preacher prophesied that one good opportunity is coming his way and he must grab it without hesitating about his age which was 50.

He was going through newspapers and on one Sunday, he came across an ad about techno- commercial manager for a Bangalore based defense procurement company. Promptly he applied and met the MD who came to Hyderabad for interview. With his background in HAL got appointed immediately with a salary of 20k and promise of 15% of profit on any order he would bring.

He was given money to get a desktop with internet connection and promptly set to work. His job was to search the internet for defense related tenders and forward them to the HO at Bangalore who will go through and send two bids: one commercial and another technical bid. In his line of work he had to visit all the defense undertakings and labs to meet the officers and submit the papers. He had to visit BHEL, ECIL and all the DRDO labs spread all around Hyderabad.

That day a German Principal is visiting to be taken to DMRL for meeting. To impress his MD and the visitor JR was using a nice dress every day. He had given one pair for laundry the previous day and in the morning as usual went buy a newspaper. After getting the paper, he returned to his home but instead of turning into his block, he went straight to the laundry about 200 meters away.

He reached the laundry and the lady was brushing her teeth outside. After seeing JR she went inside to get his clothes and came out with a plastic cover. As soon as the lady went inside three guys, two burly persons on motor bikes and one short one on a moped swooped down on him. The shorty must have be an informer, JR surmised later.

All three surrounded him and JR was perplexed and did not understand the reason. Then slowly it dawned upon him the guys are on a mission to catch him red handed in an act of espionage. It looked like they were having a wet dream of smashing an espionage ring and being rewarded with promotions and medals.

The plot involved a suspected terrorist, defense industry, a white man and finally a honeypot to spice up the narrative. JR knows he is always on their radar ever since his wayward ex-wife got into a running battle with the honey trap planted by SN Yadav.

But as soon as they saw that the lady came out with a plastic bag containing a pair of clothes, their jaws fell open and whatever they were about to bark suddenly got stuck in their throats. Their mouths uttered a guttural sound and they fled on their two wheeler as fast as they swooped down onto him. The midget followed them on his moped with a whimper.

JR was utterly confused but on seeing the three sleuths fleeing on their bikes, he burst out laughing. He was amused at their utter stupidity. Why would a terrorist exchange secret documents in broad daylight while he had all the time in the night?

He was about call to taunt them but he remembered the Goddess's warning on earlier occasions. "Never mock them". Then he remembered another incident back in his home town in Karnataka state.

During their exile to Karnataka state where they were taking shelter in their in-laws place, JR was forced to use the almost dried up High Level Canal for washing his clothes. There was only one bathroom for seventeen people and so one morning, JR packed his clothes and started walking to the canal which is around one kilometer from their place. He plodded along the rocky way to the canal in the simmering heat of summer morning sun. He got down to the bottom and started soaking his clothes in ankle deep water.

After half an hour or so, a burly gentleman obviously a cop, went by a motor cycle on the banks of the canal. He reached the railway bridge nearby and got down. He went around the bridge inspecting the tracks and the pillars. Then he walked over the spans crossing the bridge from one end to another. As he couldn't find anything suspicious, he returned to the bike and started it. JR was watching all this from the ankle deep water at the bottom of the canal. While returning, he saw JR and froze. He stopped his bike and called up someone to assure them, whoever it might be that the bridge is safe; JR was amused. He marveled at the stupidity of the cop. Why would any terrorist in his right mind would try to blow up a bridge after day break when he had all the time in the world to do it in the night?

It shows they are paranoid and they are expecting him to plant bombs or blow bridges when he had never indulged in such activity any time in his life time. One thing is extremely clear: they hold him in high regard for whatever he never thought of. Their expectations are the by-products of fertile professional criminal minds.

Back in Hyderabad, he was regularly submitting the bids and attending the opening in defense labs. All the bids of his company were on higher side, sometimes nearly three times the lowest one, and so not even a single bid was successful.

After six months the MD started grumbling about uselessness of his presence in Hyderabad. He said the he would rather manage this work from Bangalore and would visit Hyderabad by Rajdhani every week making his job at Hyderabad redundant. He was on notice to be fired if no bid is accepted in immediate future.

Due to some entrenched sources the company used to get regular business from some labs. He scoured the net frantically and zeroed on one tender of Nuclear Fuel Complex, which looked like a winner. He contacted the scientist at NFC and met him in person. He got details of the tender along with the contact details of the scientist. He downloaded the file and taken a printout. Next Sunday he visited Sarah Naidu, the preacher and after the prayers, gave her the printouts to be blessed. She took one look at the paper and said "You won't get it"

He was utterly shocked and heart broken. If this bid is not successful, he would be thrown out of the job and finding another job at his age is near impossible. He was devastated and came back to his home.

The next day early morning, he daughter who is some sort of a psychic told that last night one light came down in her room and said "Your father is cursing me for not answering his prayers. Sarah Naidu is full of negativity but I will bless the tender. Only catch is that that MD will not pay your father the promised commission but I will save your father's job."

After listening to the revelation, JR was more shocked than sorry. How can that fellow avoid paying the promised 15% commission of profit when it is clearly written in the appointment letter? The worth of the contract was about 65 lakhs rupees. 6.5 million INR. His commission on the profit would work out to around 1.5 lakh INR.

The bid went through, the MD the scientist had a meeting online and the tender was awarded to his company. When the MD visited Hyderabad next time JR gently reminded him about the promised commission.

The MD said, "Why should I pay you? I contacted the scientist directly and clinched the deal. Your role in this contract is nil."

JR did not argue but shocked at the injustice of it all. He knew that person would pay a heavy price but kept quiet. He knew the futility of arguing and trying to convince that person. Both his parents died within one year. That is another story for another day.

Slowly the MD started grumbling again about no successful tenders. Time to quit that job, he thought. One summer night, he had a terrible vision. A huge snake almost like Anaconda came down through the roof of his apartment as though it didn't exist and lifted him by a winter cap on his head. He was terrified at the sight and screaming in sleep. He thought it is coming to bite him but he was wrong. It gently lifted him by the cap.

He woke up wondering about the meaning of the dream. Why would anyone wear a winter cap in summer? He knew that he is under intense surveillance but unable to do anything about it. It all started when the SN Yadav launched a campaign of hate against his family.

His job took him to defense labs and meeting with all those scientists. It is just part of his job and no secrets were sought or exchanged. All communications were open and transparent.

The harassment from the Bangalore guy was increasing day by day. Then he saw an ad for faculty in Orissa and applied. Surprisingly he was selected for a senior faculty post in Orissa and promptly took it. After collecting his salary, he joined the new post where he was given accommodation in a flat. He noticed that while boarding the train at Secunderabad, one gentleman in plain clothes joined his compartment at the last minute.

He reached Brahmapur next day afternoon and all the agencies were on high alert upon his arrival. When after reporting to work at the institute, he was given an apartment for accommodation. When he retired for the night and switched off the lights. There was a dumb phone call and when he answered it no body responded. That might be their way of reminding him that they are watching him which was fine with him. They could have made him disappear without any trace but he remembered the Goddess promise of protecting him at all times.

Unknown to him, that place was a hotbed of insurgency and the B team was convinced that he had come there to take over command.

It all started when the team leader of A team launched his hate campaign soon after the birth of his daughter. When she was three months old, his family went to visit a temple. While returning their auto rickshaw hit one drunk crossing the road and went under a bus coming from the opposite reaction. His mother-in-law suffered a pelvic fracture and bed ridden for three months. The baby was crying nonstop and the doctor at the nearby hospital thoroughly examined the baby for any injuries and found none. Yet the baby was crying non-stop for two days. A psychic told him that it was the handiwork of SN Yadav who took an instant hatred of him and the baby. It was the first murder attempt on the child when she was only three months old.

The team leader SN Yadav was a typical worker in a government industry. He would punch in at 8.30 in the morning and after partaking tea from the canteen would go around the factory conducting his finance and cloth business. He would walk into any building without any permission as all the security guys are his customers. He sells military canteen liquor of the security people and so on a first name terms with all of them.

After partaking the subsided sumptuous lunch meant for first shift, he would go out to the city for conducting his "real estate" business. Though he couldn't convert square yards into square feet, he managed his business and made money too.

After failure of the first murder attempt, he would pass by the quarter occupied by JR twice a day. In the night, some coconut and lemons smeared with vermilion were to be seen planted by unknown persons in front of his quarter. There would be mysterious illness and money disappearing from the house.

This went on for some years and as the girl was growing up, this SN Yadav would visit her school. When she reached 7th standard, he started a smear campaign about her: that she is going around with boys on their bikes and not attending classes. The principal called her to the office and gave her a dressing down. Shocked, she told JR about this incident and he promptly rushed to the principal's office. There everyone became aware of this SN Yadav's hate campaign. JR was about file a police complaint which was dropped when the principal begged him not to go ahead and spoil the reputation of the school.

Later JR regretted for letting that person go scot free when there was a golden chance but was waiting for his next move.

The following is the table of characteristics of both A team, the originator of hate crime and B team the one tasked with the protection and safety of the country from assorted criminals and saboteurs.

A team	B team
Johnny Relevant's daughter was born on 29th May a premature baby weighing only 750 grams and the doctors at Nilofer Hospital advised him to expose the baby to morning Sun for half an hour every along with vitamin drops. When she was 3 months old, the family of JR, his wife and her mother	They are overburdened and hardworking lot. They are always ever vigilant and on the lookout for saboteurs and other threats to the security of the nation. When A team launched a hate crime trying to implicate Johnny Relevant in a honey trap case playing the victim, they pounced on the god

visited Yadagiri gutta, a famous temple near Hyderabad. After an overnight stay, they returned to Hyderabad by bus. At Jubilee bus stand, the hired an auto to return to their home at Balanagar. It was 15th August a holiday and the baby was less than three months. She was in the lap of his mother in law and the auto was driven at great speed. On the road nearer his home, a drunk suddenly lurched in front of the auto and to avoid hitting that drunk, the driver went to the extreme right and rammed it onto an oncoming city bus. In the headlong collision, the front part of the auto was smashed. The baby fortunately fell onto the bag containing clothes which cushioned her fall. But she was crying nonstop and all of them were rushed to the nearby BBR Hospital. The doctor after thoroughly examining the baby declared that there were no injuries on the child. But his mother in law had pelvic fracture and JR himself had and head injury which was not life threatening. His mother in law was admitted to the same hospital and was bedridden for three months. The child was crying inconsolably which might be due the shock of the collision.

given opportunity to find some link to the antinational. When JR was summoned to the Balanagar Police station, he went alone with his six year old daughter. There he was given a mouthful of expletives by the SHO which he heard stoically. The ungodly bitch who started it all ran away leaving him alone with the child. So he walked in but before reaching the PS he made a detour to his friends quarter who joined him at the PS. Enquires were made by the personnel where his friend Yadagiri disclosed that the waiter's daughter is spreading rumours about JR visiting her which turned out to be false. The talisman given by Ruknuddin Khalkhamkar was in his pocket. And he could feel his presence in the PS. Then the issue turned into one of catfight between the women and JR was let off with a warning and was told to give an undertaking not to harass that "innocent "girl in future. That goes for his bitch of a wife too. So he signed the undertaking and returned home. He could see the leader of A team walking around the PS keen to know how his plan was unfolding. Little did JR know that B team would open a dossier on his six year old

Fourteen years when the hand of that SN Yadav became obvious in the planned destruction of his family, JR got a medium from Ranigunj for consultation. That medium told him to take him near the quarter of that SN Yadav's in HAL Township. So he got that swamiji in his car and drove in front of quarter occupied in the township. While passing in front that house, the medium told him that that SN Yadav started practising black magic exactly fourteen years and three months ago. When JR calculated the date it came to exactly 15th August 1989 the day their auto rickshaw collided into an oncoming city bus. That was the first murder attempt on his daughter when she was less than three months old. JR could not understand the intensity of hatred from an unknown Andhra villager who also migrated to the city in search of lively hood. There was a theft in a house occupied by him when the child was one year old in which all the valuables were physically stolen leaving only the documents intact which were by the grace of the goddess were not lost. As she was growing up this SN Yadav would make rounds of her school and started planting daughter and four cops would be placed under suspension twenty years later. When the instructions given by the Goddess were followed by JR, he was offered a voluntary retirement plan which he grabbed to come out of the job at HAL so as to get out of defence industry. With the proceeds of the settlement he purchased a sick engineering industry with the blessings of his guru. The seller took him to Delhi to buy brass pins for three pin electrical plugs. In Delhi the cost was Rs 1.50 a pair where as in Hyderabad, it was Rs 6.50 a pair. The value addition was good and after paying the money, the supplier would send the consignment to his address at Hyderabad. He returned home and waited and waited. The consignment didn't arrive and upon enquiry was told that the truck was impounded at Madhya Pradesh and thorough scrutiny was being done on the manifest as to the contents and source. It seems that particular transporter had never encountered such scrutiny. It seems B team suspected some contraband or ingredients for WMD in that truck. Anyway, JR felt a dark cloud had fallen on his unit and it would collapse in due time.

stories of his daughter bunking classes and moving around boys in their motor bikes. When the principal called and reprimanded her, she cried and rushed to home to inform JR. He went to the principal and gave her a piece of his mind. The principal upon realising the story as fake, begged JR not to go ahead and not to file a police complaint. JR kept quiet and waited for that criminal to make his next move.

Proxy punching, free roaming bootlegging and pimping are the main activities of this team leader by name B Sathya Narayana Yadav. He would punch in at 8.30 in the morning and go around the factory selling plots, clothes and household items in the factory premises. Since he also deals with the business of selling defence issue liquor of the security guards who are mostly from defence forces, all the guards are his friends and so don't bother of asking for movement pass while he roams all the buildings of the factory. It seems this person hails from a family practising black magic. After partaking the sumptuous highly subsidised lunch at 1030 meant for first shift workers, he would go out to the

B team was desperately seeking WMDs in that company and used to visit in various disguises. But all they saw was workers idling with no work. Then the unit was sold at half the price closing it after paying the pending salaries to the workers.

Interim score; B team were fully involved in protecting the country from internal and external enemies. So they went on harassing JR's daughter and wife when he was working in Odisha. They would call up in the middle of the night and ask them the why they were calling them on unknown numbers. They were terrified and would switch of their phones till morning. His daughter joined a college and had to catch the first bus at 6.30 in the morning to attend the classes. Then the patrol car would rush from the police station and stop at the bus stop which used to be deserted at that time. Then they would loudly discuss on how to kidnap and rape her. They would wait till the bus arrives and would depart once she boards the bus. After the classes were over, another bunch of thugs would hound her in a patrol car at the bus stop. They did it for city to run his other businesses. After visiting his business areas he would get tired and would return to the company quarters and take a well-deserved rest. Then he would saunter into the factory along with second shift workers at 230 in the afternoon. After some more business rounds inside he would punch out at 5.15 along with general shift workers. All his wandering inside the factory are not only for business purposes. He would carry tales about people he hates particularly SC&, STs. His fertile criminal brain came up with a master plan to implicate JR in a honey trap with a canteen worker's daughter playing the role of victim. He carefully coached the girl to play victim and she started spreading calumny about JR with the womenfolk of the township.

JR had a powerful Sufi saint at Wadi who saved him many times earlier. He warned JR not to react to the honey trap's calumny as merely speaking to her would lead him to certain death. Such was the evil about that that honey trap. But JR's wife was an ungodly woman who didn't bother about the warnings by Ruknuddin Khalkamkar. To her any woman is a game for a some days until she got terrified and drop out of college. When JR returned home on leave, she narrated the issue and he didn't know how to face it. Later he came across a news item where on ASI and four cops were placed under suspension for using third on a person in a civil dispute. JR didn't give it much thought until one day an old woman in church told him" I have taken care of those who harassed your daughter. Post this message in your Facebook page." He complied and the B team stopped harassing the woman folk Glory to the Goddess.

quarrel and had a running battle with that honey trap and the canteen worker's daughter would constantly brag about getting JR beaten in police lockup on some cooked up charges. By constantly goading her, SN Yadav made her lodge a complaint orally with the Balanagar police station. One fine day he was summoned and SN Yadav was filled with glee at the process of success of his plan. Unknown to that gang, Ruknuddin Khalkhamkar, his guru was watching over him and saved him from their evil plans.

SN Yadav was seething with rage as his carefully scripted plan of third degree did not materialize All his bragging with his friends inside factory did not materialise. He was desperately looking for a suitable means to destroy and kill all the members of JR family.

After getting the offer of VRS, JR vacated the quarters and took residence at Ramarajanagar on the way to Medchal. Then he came to know about the celebrations by the A team and SN Yadav distributing sweets worth fifty thousand rupees in the factory. Then he located the unit on Kukatpally highway during his trips outside the factory. His favourite weapon was unleashed on the company so the unit went sick unable to pay electricity bills. The unit was put up for sale and there were no takers. During his visits to Hospet town, he spoke to one of street side fortune tellers who made him throw dice when asked about his unit. He said you bought that unit trusting a divine power but it was turned into a grave yard by two persons: one black faced and the other brown faced one. Then after taking some money he gave a talisman and was told to keep it in the pooja room. The unit would be sold in one week time and the buyer would come from the western direction of that company.

JR came to the city and complied with it. The unit was sold not in one week but after two weeks at less than half the price it was purchased. All the pending salaries were paid and his family hit the road.

Interim score: JR family was taking shelter at a place on the Medchal highway and A team leader tracked them successfully. So he started visiting the people nearby and spreading canards. That he duped many people and owes money to everyone, that he had been imprisoned etc. JR heard these gossip and at that time he was regularly attending the prayer meetings of a single mother by name Sarah Naidu. In one meeting he told all the canards that person spreading around his neighbourhood. She told him to get a poach of drinking water, the type they sell for one rupee in all provision stores. He purchased it and after prayer, she touched the water sachet and told to cut the sachet and throw the contents anywhere in that place of residence. He came home and waited for the evening to perform that mission. Then he went to Balanagar and to the HAL township. It became dark by the time he reached the township and that person's quarters. He cut open the water sachet and threw it in that compound leaving the judgement to the divine. Later he came to know the eldest daughter was beaten to death by her husband, the other one's husband died in an accident and third one was deserted by her husband.

After being hit there was no change of heart on the part of SN Yadav and he became more determined to destroy JR and his family: they are of a stubborn race.

During his journeys to Hyderabad and back, cops would watch his berth in train and shine torches to confirm his presence when he was sleeping. Once a lady passenger asked him about it and he smiled and said "I too don't know the reason."

After spending two years in Brahmapur, the third year, while coming to the institute in the morning, he heard a voice in his ear saying" You would leave after Nag Chavithi". It is the festival of serpents as per Hindu calendar. At his desk he looked up the calendar and found that Nag Chavithi comes around August. So he braced for the departure. That day came and went but nothing happened. That day happened to be Nag Panchami which is celebrated in some parts of the country

After August came and went the voice spoke again repeating the same message. Then he found that the actual Nag Chavithi falls after Diwali. And that year it was on 15th November.

Three months before the expiry of the contract he was told that he has to leave on November 15 which happened to the Day of Nag Chavithi. He smiled to himself at the fulfilment of the prophesy.

Then he returned to Hyderabad and started looking for some jobs but not very successful. He got some low paying jobs off and on.

Later after some days, he had a dream in which a voice told him "Watch this scene in Pet Basheerabad police station." Pet Basheerabad is the place where the police station is located bearing that name. In that scene he was suspended upside down and some burly cops were beating with sticks to find the location of bombs allegedly planted by him. As they were beating him they were shouting "Where are the bombs?"

Then he realized the true meaning of the dream of Anaconda diving from heavens to rescue him from Hyderabad. Apparently all his movements in defense industries were for recon purpose and as per their fertile criminal brains, he was planning to pull out a mega lone wolf terrorists strike.

They were beating with canes all while shouting "Where are the bombs.?

All the while, the goddess was watching over him and just before they could swoop down on him, she pulled him out of Hyderabad and its defense industry. The focus shifted to Maoists of Orissa of which JR has no clue. Yet they could have taken him into custody and given their favorite treatment to implicate in some conspiracy. He was sensing it all the time he spent in that place. It didn't happen as the Goddess promised a ring of fire around the three of his family members.

Glory to the Goddess.

JAI HIND.

Tag words: Yadagiri gutta, Jubilee bus sand, BBR hospital, Balanagar, HAL Township

How I Killed My Mom

Fulfilment of an ancient prophesy

I was the eldest son of my parents and born after my eldest sister. My siblings are four brothers and two sisters. I was born in Jabalpur military hospital as my father was in the army. My birth certificate was signed by the military doctor a certain Capt. Phobli. Curiously though none of my parents were associated with Christianity, my mother's religion was recorded as Christianity.

My mother seem to be of a certain genetic aberration as she was born devoid of any maternal instincts. She was the most pitiless woman I have ever seen in my life though I had seen several cruel women, observing her at close quarters, I could sense that she is of a different breed. She would like to beat the kids at the slightest provocation yet that didn't stop me from indulging in waywardness. She would like to wake us up by five with the morning with a first round of beating with her favorite stick which she used to keep handy near the attic. I could sense that the stress of bringing up a large family on a soldiers pay which was around 90 rupees in those days was having a terrible on her mental health.

While not deployed in family stations, she used to be residing near her mom's place. The long years of separation took a heavy toll on her mental wellbeing. Though I am sympathetic towards her in retrospect, I could not stomach the needless cruelty towards her own children. While beating us all collectively in one session, I used to shield my siblings from her by covering them which she used to watch with great astonishment. She never appreciated kindness in any one and her tongue lashing was just that, like a lash from a whip.

One particular incident is strongly etched in my mind. As s toddler, I had a boil on my thigh which was swollen and was very painful. I was the legendary cry baby and was crying all the time. She carried me to the military hospital where the doctor gave some liquid and a cream to be applied to the boil. After coming out of the dispensary, she took me to the washroom, and crushed the boil with her bare hands. It burst with blood and pus oozing out. I was hollering in great pain which she ignored. Then she threw the ointment and medicine in dust bin and returned home. The boil healed eventually but at great cost of my pain.

When not deployed in family stations, my dad would come home on leave of two months at a stretch which was a nightmare to all of us. She would maintain a record of all the acts of mischief of us especially of mine as I was a wayward one. His arrival on leave would get us terrified as she would recite all of my omissions and commissions. We would be spending our days under the trees to escape beatings from his side.

After he is gone I would be planning to run away from this hell of a place. Once I got into a train going to Secunderabad, but after few minutes into the journey, I got cold feet and got down at a wayside station. It was very dark with no lights, and one gang man found me loitering in the dark deserted platform. When enquired about my presence, I bluffed that I got into a wrong train while all of my family went away by another one.

He didn't believe me but appeared convinced. He made me sleep on a cot nearby and told me that he would put me back on any train that comes that night. After many hours, a goods train came and the gang man spoke to the fireman of the steam locomotive when he came to the station master's office. So I got into the steam locomotive and reached my place around 2.30 in the night. I got down from the running locomotive as it did not stop at the station.

Back at home more lies about my absence as I told my mom about studying at my classmates place. She ignored me altogether but the beatings continued as usual.

Then I met another friend by name Hanumanth reddy in my class. He was from a rich background but some reason planning to run away from home. Boys of certain age do that all the time mostly from dysfunctional families. But my friend didn't have any issues at home.

Yet all the time he was discussing the same topic while sitting on a nearby railway track. He was planning to runaway to Bangalore and work in any hotel while I was hell bent on completing school education. One day he gave me the ultimatum and told he was running away that night itself. I too was ready to join him.

So we met in the evening at the railway station and Hanumanth reddy got two tickets to Bangalore. The train started and my friend promptly went to sleep on the floor. When the train reached I had second thoughts as I must obtain my school certificate at any cost.

So I woke up my friend and told him to get to get two tickets back to our pace which he rushed and got them. The return train was on the next platform and we promptly got in. Hanumanth reddy promptly went to sleep on the floor and we reached our town back in the same night. After reaching the station, Hanumanth reddy went back his home and reached my place of horrors in the same night. That way my second attempt also ended in a fiasco.

My mom was violent all the time and always grumbling about provisions like rice and oil which use to run out as she had to feed the five of us in the meagre salary of my dad. To earn extra money she used to stitch clothes for the women folk of our locality. She used to save the coins in a piggy bank which I found out and was stealing regularly to eat outside.

Fights were regular in our home and she used to remind me that she would meet her death at my hands as one swamiji prophesied at the time of my birth. Killing a woman that too one's own mother was unthinkable for me.

I was a wayward fellow and was not afraid of the local bullies. One vegetable vendor, by name Pendekanti Booma was a fearsome woman of our locality. Everyone was afraid of her and none dared to pick up a fight with her. Her grandson was a local bully and one day our paths crossed. I had a wrestling match with that bully and threw him down to ground. He went away hollering to his grand ma and she came out mouthing obscenities at me, the tormentor of her beloved grandson.

My mom came out to attack her and there was a full scale war between them and I knew the consequences. So I ran away and went on loitering around the village hoping things would cool down in the meantime. I returned in the evening hoping she might have cooled down a bit but a grand welcome was awaiting for me. I was given good thrashing with her favourite stick and went bed whimpering at the beatings.

Things became worse after my father retired from the army and had an agriculture land of 10 acres which had gone fallow as it was not cultivated in his absence. My parents were made for each other type in cruelty as my dad put me to work as free labor in construction of our home and also ploughing the land. He was a pitiless slave driver. My work output was equal to five labors and he used me as free labor. I was working for food and my education was always in my focus.

After seven years of hard labor, I obtained a degree from the local college. Then I took a leap of faith and as advised by a north Indian friend, prayed to Ma Vaishno Devi to make me an engineer.

To cut a long story short, the Goddess, got me the degree in engineering and I started to seek work in Hyderabad. Meanwhile my father died and I was driven out by my mom.

I got married to an unknown girl from my home town and we were moving around seeking job and shelter. Then I got a government job which I felt was a blessing from the divine.

Hyderabad was the capital for the undivided Andhra Pradesh and thousands migrated to that city from all over the state.

One particular migrant from coastal Andhra took an immediate dislike to me: it was hate at first sight and I didn't realize it at that time. Unknown to me that person belongs to a family of black magicians. He used to practice his trade on other worker who are financially better off. His gaze fell on me and my daughter and he hated her for no apparent reason. He is a migrant from coastal Andhra and we were from Karnataka state.

He was stealing our money so that my daughter could not get good education. He would visit her school when she was in 7th standard and spread rumors about her moving with boys on their bikes and going to movies.

This person was burning with hatred towards us and we lost all our assets. That person made us bankrupt and we were unable to pay rent. So I pulled her out of school, locked out our flat and left for our in laws place. I have to dispose of a flat on which I have taken housing finance. I tried to dispose of the flat and repay the finance company but that turned to be a herculean task.

I was advertising in papers regularly and many shady characters were looking at that place but turning it down.

I was told that someone had done black magic on that house so that all three of us would die there by committing suicide.

Then impressed by the testimonies on TV, I started attending Christian churches only to dispose of that flat. Many months of fasting, praying and paying tithes the flat was finally sold off at great loss.

Even after so much praying and fasting, no jobs came my way and we were not able to pay rent for many months.

While staying at our in laws place, I went around and found a tea stall. I sat down on the bench to have tea and observed a Catholic picture in that place. I asked Yesu, the tea stall owner about it. He said it sold at the Church at Harihara, a small town in Karnataka state where Mother Mary appeared to heal a Brahmin of leprosy. He also said a preacher by name Francis visits his place very often. He told me to wait for that Francis as he was a chosen one and has great spiritual powers.

Meanwhile the preacher was boarding a bus to Uravakonda, another small town near Ananthapur, the district headquarters. While getting into the bus he heard a voice telling him to go back as a family is in great distress.

So he came back Hospet and I met him at Yesus's tea stall. Then he told us to accompany him Sindhanur where he conducts prayer meetings. I alone agreed to join him and we reached Sindhanur.

Accommodation was provided for me and others also. Food was also provided free of cost and we prayed all day, In the night I was told to sleep in the same room with Francis. This continued for three days and on the third day I was told to go back to our place.

So I left after lunch, confused as the preacher did not give any verse or prophesy. I was depressed and came back to our town. As I was loitering in that town, my mom sent word through an acquaintance to meet her.

So I went to meet her. She had a stroke and her speech was blurred. She had hard time recollecting names. With some effort she conveyed to me to come to the registrar office the next day as she wished to give a part of the property to me. I replied I don't need her property and I am willing to forego my share in lieu of money.

Then my brothers happily grabbed that chance and I got money enough to pay towards outstanding rent.

I collected the money came back to Hyderabad paid the overdue rent. That church near Sindhanur became our refuge when I was unemployed and homeless.

During one visit, the preacher Francis gave the following verses to recite twice a day for 85 days.

1. Sirach 23:20 to 22

2. Wisdom 12:12 to 21

3. Sirach 28: 1

4. Jeremiah 11:1

5. 1 Samuel 15:10

6. Psalms 10

7. Joel 21:13

8. Nahum 1:3

9. Mathew11:28

10. Acts 12:6 to 19

He would sit in front of the altar and write down the verses. When dictating these verses, he didn't mention the purpose and being very disciplined and obedient, I too didn't argue about it.

So I started reciting these verses duty fully twice a day as instructed and on 85th day I received a phone call informing about the death of my mother. All our relatives were jubilant as her death took place on the day of Vaikunta Ekadasi where the gates of heaven are thrown open. Many Hindus seek death on that particular day as they are assured of their passage to heaven on that particular day. Also it is observed that very few accidents take place on that day usually nobody dies in those accidents.

But I had my own misgivings and went to a preacher near Marredpally. He told me to bring me a photo of my mom and also the photo of my younger brother's son.

I returned home and got the photos from and old album. I visited the pastor with the photos and he took them. He closed his eyes and seemed to have gone to sleep. Then he opened his eyes and said this boy murdered that old woman for money.

I was shocked beyond belief. My younger brother has a son who is a vagrant. Even after spending huge money on his education, he cannot read even a wall poster. He was living off her property and disposing off her valuable for an easy life. He used to snatch her pension and make merry. In case the old woman resists, he would beat her black and blue.

Contrary to the popular myth she was killed on the previous day of Vaikunta Ekadasi.

I alone knew the secret of her death as she used to mention prophesy of a swami long ago very often. She used to say that her death would take place at my hands as predicted by a holy man at the time of my birth. That ancient prophecy manifested albeit in a different way.

PS; The church where Francis used to preach is between Sindhanur and Bellary at a place called Sirigere cross roads. It was a thatched hut built in the midst of agricultural lands. One acre of land was donated by a devotee to build that church and it is away from the main road by one kilometer.

Once I visited the church at Sirigere for an overnight stay. While sleeping in the church, I had a dream in which many people are sitting before a throne may be waiting to be heard or sentenced I was not sure. Then I saw my mom and she asked me "Why have done this to me?"

I replied "Sorry mother, I was only obeying God's command."

Later I was told that she was into black magic to kill us and make my daughter an orphan. Dear readers, do you believe that I am guilty of matricide?

Please pray for forgiveness if you believe I am guilty.

Tag words: Pastor Francis, Bellary, Sindhanur, Sirigere cross

Huligamma Devi at Munirabad in Karnataka State

Three of our families of went on a tour of Karnataka State. As we heard much about the glorious ruins of Hampi, we wished to visit that place first. That city was highly praised by European travelers for its riches. All 12 of us taken a mini bus on hire and started from Hyderabad. After visiting the vast expanse of the ruins which were leisurely destroyed for more than six months by the victors of Talikota war, we felt much depressed at the loss of a magnificent Hindu kingdom. The guide explained to us a strange tale for the sudden end of that kingdom.

It seems when Sage Vidyaranya prayed for wealth to build a magnificent kingdom, gold was showered from sky for 7 Ghadiyas. I am not sure of that unit of measurement of time and the guide was also clueless. It can be safely assumed that much wealth was showered from heaven to build a kingdom. To lay foundation of the fort, an auspicious time called muhurat in Hindu parlance has to be fixed which lays strong foundation for any venture. So the Sage calculated one such moment and told Hari Hara and Bukka Raya to start digging the foundation for the fort at the time indicated by him. He told them that he will be meditating on the hill and blow a conch as signal for the correct time to start digging. So they all assembled at the chosen place and after performing puja, the swami went up the hill. The disciples were eagerly waiting for the signal and as soon as they heard it, they started digging for the foundation. After some more time another conch sound was heard, they were confused and stopped working.

Later the swami came down and enquired whether they followed his signal. They replied that they started digging at the first call and stopped at the second signal. Swamiji denied he gave two signals with the conch and proceeded to verify about any other call. It turned out the first call was blown in a funeral procession and second one was that of the swami. He was heartbroken and calculated again based on the first signal. He declared that the rule of this kingdom shall last only 200 years instead of 2000 years as calculated and it shall end suddenly after that. It was all in the cosmic way of things or we would have another independent kingdom even after India becoming free from the British rule.

After visiting Hampi and worshipping at the Virupaksha temple which mysteriously escaped destruction at hands of the victors. There are different versions on how the temple escaped destruction while all others were destroyed. One version is as the soldiers of Bahamani sultans were mostly Shaivaites, worshippers of Shiva, they spared the Virupaksha temple; another version is as they were attacking it wild boars came out of the temple to protect it and so the attackers fled from that place.

Pujas are being performed even now right from the time of Vijayanagara kingdom. Next day we visited the Tungabhadra Dam which is a joint venture between AP and Karnataka Governments. It is a major dam with a capacity of 100 TMC against 200TMC of Srisailam and 300TMC of Nagarjunasagar dam further down.

Then someone mentioned a temple further downstream after the dam some seven kilometers away. So we went by our minibus after having our lunch in the park below the dam. That place is called Munirabad but the temple itself is called Huligi. We parked our vehicle washed our feet after depositing our footwear and entered the temple with offering of coconuts and green bangles. There was no idol but image in relief in granite called Shri Chakra. While all others went to play in the river which had only water up to knees and as there is no danger of drowning I let them have their way. Then I came back and sat down in the mantap for devotees and turned to my side and saw a well-dressed gentleman in his fifties. I asked him about the temple and can he kindly agreed to act as our guide. He was speaking fluent English and readily agreed.

He said the origins of the temple are rooted in antiquity. There were two brothers, great devotees of Saudatti Yellamma, near Belgaum. They were performing pooja to Saudatti Yellamma every year during the month of Sravan. As there was no dam to control the river Tungabhadra, it was fully in spate overflowing the banks. They were unable to cross the river and much depressed. The Devi appeared to them in a vision and told them she had taken the shape of Sri Chakra and is right at the bottom of the present temple. They were told to perform the pooja at that place itself and the brothers were overjoyed. So they built a small temple as it stands today." said our guide.

He continued "it was also mentioned at the time of Tipu Sultan. It seems when Tipu invaded the tiny kingdom the chieftain was terrified and had no way of facing the mighty army of Tipu and also he could not meet the demand of tribute. He cloistered himself inside the temple and crying his heart out pleading to the Goddess to save his people as Tipu's cruelty was legendary. He would spare none and slaughter anyone not surrendering to him.

"As the chieftain pleading in the temple one night, a lady in white passed through Tipu's camp. A furious tempest tore through the camp uprooting tents and making horses run amok. Then she sent message to Tipu through the commander of the army to leave that place without troubling her devotee. Tipu agreed to go back and the chief was saved from horrible outcome from an unjust war thrust upon him.

I said "That was some centuries ago. What about recent past? The gentleman pointed to a row of coconut trees and said" You see the row of coconut trees after the temple?"

I said "Yes" He said "They are graves of Razakars killed by Indian army in police action during liberation of Hyderabad. You see this was part of Hyderabad province and the Nizam refused to accede to the Indian Union. A reign of terror was let loose by followers of Kasim Razvi popularly known as Razakars. Murder rape and mayhem were let loose by them and when Army moved firing at all and sundry many hundreds were killed. Some Razakars taking advantage of the chaos hid under a pile of corpses inside the temple. Spirit of the goddess came onto the priest who in turn informed army personnel. The hiding Razakars were found under pile of corpses just as told by the priest, were pulled out and shot dead. They were buried here and coconut trees were planted on the site. You can see the graves even now.

Shankar said "You see the trans genders playing single string instruments."

I replied "Yes"

He said "One of them was a Sub Inspector of police and one an automobile workshop owner" I asked "What happened them?"

He said "They were alpha males but unfortunately they committed sacrilege with the Goddess. They were mocking her temple and other Transgenders. After several warnings, she emasculated them. Masculinity cannot be taken for granted" I was shocked beyond belief.

"After the Hyderabad acceded to Indian Union, trains were running from Guntakal to Hubli on meter gauge railway track. You see the railway bridge over there on the river Tungabhadra? Now it is converted to broad gauge. Steam engines were the prime movers in those days. After liberation of Hyderabad, the temple was in ruins with not many visitors. Then one day a passenger train pulled by steam locomotive stopped on the railway bridge for no apparent reason. Engineers from Guntakal and Hubli were rushed to fix whatever problem with the engine but they could not figure out the problem. Then spirit of the Goddess came onto a lady and told them that her temple is ruins and she won't permit trains to run by ignoring her temple. When the Government promised to repair the temple and sanctioned funds, the train started moving.

Tag words: Saudatti Yellamma, Munirabad Dam, Sage Vidyaranya, Talikota war.

Close Encounter with God

A tribute to the dedication of Indian police in defending the country from enemies

Johnny Relevant was sleeping in his bed on the floor in his apartment after supper after his contract expired and he returned Hyderabad. He got some low paying temporary jobs and most of his time spent in applying for some vacancies he found in newspapers. He realized that experience does not count much as only freshers have a chance of finding a job in the market.

It was only 930 in the night and he could clearly hear the TV in the hall. Then he sensed a reptile slithering on the calf of his right foot. He was not afraid but only curious about it. As snake slid on his calf, it suddenly bit him. He could sense venom entering his body and life ebbing away. It was a pleasant experience while it lasted, then he woke up and came into the hall where his daughter was watching TV. He said "I had a terrible experience." His daughter asked "What was it about? "He replied "I was bitten by a snake in bed just now." She was thoughtful and kept quiet.

He was certain that a momentous event had taken place but didn't know what it was. He sat before the computer and began searching the answer to this mysterious event. Different religions gave different versions and none had a satisfactory answer. According to some it was a good omen and some it was not so.

Then his daughter who is a crypto psychic said "your power to earn money is taken away. In the Bible heel is the support system on which your very being is based." That was the real meaning of the attack as he applied for hundreds of ads got selected for some only to be dropped out next day for no apparent reason. There was no money to pay rent and whatever they got by tuition fees was used up to buy provisions. A spirit of suicide was hovering over him. His daughter and her mom were cursing him for not earning any money and told him that he is better off dead than be a parasite feeding off their earnings.

He was planning to end it all leaving them to their fates but that is exactly what A team was planning; murder by suicide. After he departs from this world wolves of both A and B team will have a field day torturing them but God put him in charge of their lives and commanded to protect them at all costs. So he was hanging on to life ignoring the insults as he believed in his visions shown during meditation.

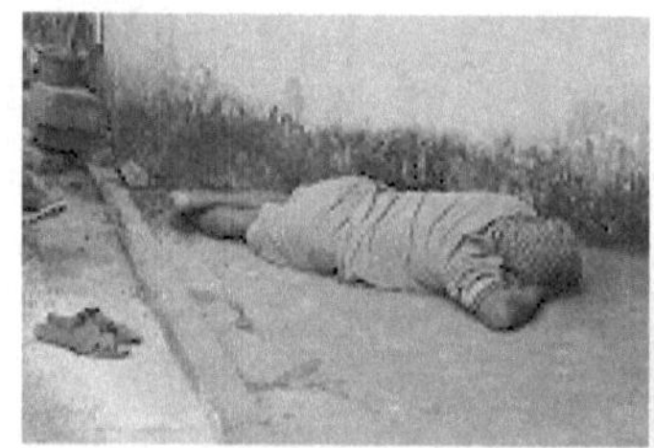

He sought refuge in Christianity but was disappointed as none of the verses manifested. No amount of fasting, praying, paying tithes and confessing brought about any change. On a visit to YMCA to attend a sermon by a supposedly powerful preacher to listen to the usual bombastic prophesies which never manifest.

One gentleman whose son playing in the basketball court met him and advised him to meet a swami at an ashram between Kalwakurthy and Nagarkurnool about 100 kilometers s from the city.

He collected some money and boarded the bus one early morning. After changing over to another bus at Kalwakurthy, he boarded another bus to Nagarkurnool and after half an hour later he reached the ashram. The ashram turned out to be a serene place half a kilometer away from the main road. As he made his way by walk towards the ashram, he knew the B team must be on his tail. They never give up and trying to monitor his movements even to the toilet and the purpose in not known. He is on a higher level of undesirables on their list and they don't give up on watching wherever he goes. One visit to the local police station on 11th Sep 1996 set the whole security apparatus tailing him ever since.

A team set up a honey trap in the form of a waiter's daughter who went on claiming to have an affair with JR and claiming to spend all his free time at their shack. He only causally chatted with her on the way to get an auto to go to bus stand that too only once and didn't even know her name. The angel warned not to react whatever might be the provocation. Once he talks to her the matter goes beyond his power as the petite Greek goddess planted by A team is actually the devil in disguise.

While walking by the dirt road to the ashram, JR felt that this is the best location in case B team decides to take a hit and finish him off in a fake encounter. After intense surveillance for 20 years, they could not get anything incriminating and they were desperate to find the missing link to Osama Bin Laden due to his mentor. His spiritual god father who happened to be a Muslim from a wayside town of WADI on the border with Karnataka state.

The swami turned out to be a middle aged lady who is reputed to be on fast for last 30 years not taking even a drop of water. Before entering the ashram one has to take bath at a well away from the ashram and leave footwear outside the compound. The swami sits on a throne every week first dispensing holy water in one queue. Later she sits on the throne answering queries of the devotees. Each devotee gets hardly one minute to present his or case but even that is not really necessary as the swami herself tells them their problems and solution too and just standing in her presence is sufficient for her make her prophesies.

After observing the formalities Johnny joined the queue and his turn came after waiting for 12 hours. Such was the crowd every week.

As he stood in her presence, she said "Lakhs of rupees of your money was stolen by witchcraft and your lower abdomen was crushed. You were killed twice but God raised you from death both times. And he is trying very hard to kill you again." Swami was referring to one incident on the night of 17th Dec 2015 when one hand, just a hand up to the wrist, crawled on to the thigh and touched his testicles. In the morning, while taking bath, he noticed that the testicles have turned into pouches filled with water.

He requested the swami to bless with a job to which swami told him to visit again next Friday. He collected the holy water and returned home and immediately there was a teaching assignment from a rich family which kept the home kitchen fires burning.

After this relief, he went to pray for a job several times as promised but no job came his way He sensed someone tailing him. While during one visit, he sensed something sinister was in the air. One rooky cop in plain clothes followed him after he alighted from the rural bus.

While accosting he said, "Do you know that I am following you right from your first visit?" JR didn't answer and went on walking towards the ashram. The cop in plain clothes said" This is the fifth time I am following you".

JR ignored him and went on walking. "The rooky cop paused and it looked like he was expecting him to run. He then looked towards the bus stop and made some secret gestures with his hands. It was as if he had some back up and they both were getting ready to pounce on and overpower him in case JR start to run.

JR didn't find any reason to run and kept on walking. Finally the rooky cop got disappointed and went back to join the backup sleuth.

After several visits to the ashram, JR failed to get any job and he was hopeful about the power of the swami to bless him with a job. Then once again he chose to visit the ashram.

It was a no darshan day as it was scheduled for the weekend and it was only Monday. The ashram was deserted and he found a place to sleep. A phone call came at around midnight from an unknown number and he called back. No one responded.

He knew the B team stalking him and it looks like they are going for the final solution that night after continuous surveillance for 20 years. Johnny Relevant was glad that all that silly surveillance is coming to an

end one way or the other and eagerly looking forward for the 'encounter."
He knew there was a hit squad out in the darkness and will finish him off
before dawn. And he was glad for the B team as finally they will get some
reward for all the hard work taken up last twenty years. They must at least
get some Mahavir Chakra and accelerated promotions for all that hard
work they have put up in protecting the country.

He was relieved that in few hours he is going to meet Jesus and
other gods and discuss all their failed prophesies. The wait is over, he
was grateful for B team for sending him on this final journey and those
gentlemen richly deserve rewards for all that hard work they have put up
for more than twenty years.

As the ashram was deserted, he easily found a place to sleep and kept
his bag on the cobbled floor and went to rest.

He heard a sound like a machine gun fire and he was standing before a
bright light. JR realized he is standing before the All Embracing Light.

Then he spoke. He said "God, I am here. I am grateful for all the
angels you sent to save me right from getting me out of the encirclement
at my work place. I am here to plead for the case of B team who mounted
nonstop surveillance for twenty years in the noble cause of defending the
country, sparing no expenditure or not lacking any effort.

God asked "How did happen"?

JR replied "the woman you gave me disobeyed the commandment of
your angel not to speak to the honey trap planted by A team. She had a
running battle with that devil in disguise who was threatening to get me
arrested by police. I did not understand on what grounds. Now cops of all
shades from CBI to SBI are baying for my blood."

God said "I have heard it before."

"Yes my Lord, the disobedience of Eve brought about the downfall of
humanity.

"Your angel saved my daughter from kidnap, rape, torture and death
on her way to college when he warned about the plans of A team. I
honored your angel's words and did not send her to regular college in spite

of the great ruckus created by her mom. You blessed my obedience and praised me as 'The David who snatched the lamb from the teeth of Lion'. But the stupid bitches go on nagging about not sending her to regular college and destroying her career. Had I ignored your angel's warning, she would be dead by now which they don't realize.

"And they planted an item girl as a rich and innocent divorcee in the marriage bureau I was visiting. Your angel saved me from 'that marriage' at the last minute from that deadly informer, naxalites, spy or freelancer I am not sure whatever she was. Any way they have taken secret photos of me travelling with her and stored them for future whenever necessary.

God asked, "What is an item girl?"

He replied' Lord, an item girl is the answer to all the fantasies of an average male. But in this case she serves only cops as I saw her hobnobbing with cops in a restaurant at Shankar mutt"

"Lord as I believed to be a genuine divorcee in all my naiveté, I took her to my native place to meet my mother. That was when she flared up for no apparent reason which made me suspect her antecedents. She refused to meet my mom and I felt something is not right. A woman of shady character is terrified of meeting a housewife because only females can see through whatever façade the other one is putting up. It is a female thing. Her handlers did a lousy job of training her "After returning to the city I was tricked by the matrimony agency to marry that rich and innocent divorcee but just three days before that "marriage" your angel Ruknuddin Khalkamkhar warned me over phone that she was neither divorced nor rich and her husband is very much alive. He would come after me and my life would be terrible with both B team and naxals baying for my blood. He also warned me that B team had taken secret photos of me with her for future use. I am alive till now only due to the guidance of your angel.

"This B team has stolen video games, watch and other toys of my kid kept in the window sill, all part of their sacred duty of defending the country. They also planted an n unknown SIM in my shirt pocket in a crowded city bus. They can teach a trick or two to many agencies in the Dirty Tricks Department.

God asked "How does it work"?

"Lord just by inserting that SIM in my phone would automatically make me a member of some secret group controlled by B team. Fortunately you gave me sense not to attempt such a thing.

JR went on "Lord they opened a dossier on my daughter when she was six years old and I took her along to the police station when the bitch started it all ran away instead of defending me.

Twenty years later when I sent her to college, they harassed and threatened her and so she had to drop out of college. Our goddess took her revenge by getting those thugs placed under suspension. But I am disappointed with their mere suspension.

God said "What do you want me to do? Blow them up in a land mine blast? They won't be able to connect the dots and get enlightened."

JR: You could have get them a custodial death to meet ends of justice" and continued" I am seething with rage for making her drop out of college and forfeit the fees".

God: Look my friend, I know my Law. I understand your pain. Besides they seem to have got enlightened and not harassing your people anymore. We will review again in case they start any hanky-panky.

God asked "Why didn't you take that offer of transfer to MD's office as proposed by your GM"

JR replied "God, are you kidding? Can you imagine the ramifications? It might be the most sought after posting for a potential spy to steal all those "secrets". They would have intensified surveillance to find what secrets I might be stealing and might have invented something to finish me off. So I decided to quit once for all and take the rough road. One angel warned me that my 12 year old daughter would also be taken into custody and subjected to third degree treatment if I continued in that job. So I decided to quit and taken the rough road. Besides life would have become worthless once my child returns from that third degree treatment. I would have committed suicide unable to bear the third degree treatment given to my daughter."

"However even after quitting that job, the surveillance intensified and I was told that I left the job to take up my guru's assignment "

God asked "what might that be?'

"The security establishment suspected that my guru, Ruknuddin Khalkamkhar was running a terror module and asked me to join his group. I was offered a pay of Rupees 40 thousands for each successful hit; I got the exact figure from a medium. His Muslim name automatically made him a suspect and I am also not sure of his denomination. He used to tell me to worship Hanuman and visit Thrupathi for darshan of Lord Balaji. He was anything but a Wahhabi terrorist."

"Anyway you can't send me back to earth." I said.

God answered "Why not" Johnny said "Because my body is riddled with holes like a rag with bullets when they emptied their magazines of SLRs and their carbines. And nobody can stitch it back.

God said "Do you really think so? I am sending you back now." And he pushed him down to earth. Then he felt like he was falling down from a great height and someone shaking him. He came back to his senses and saw one attendant of the ashram shaking him violently. "Get up" he said "swami wants to talk to you."

He woke up groggy realizing the sound of gunfire he heard was only his snoring. He went and stood in front of the swami.

The Swami asked "Did you come alone?"

He replied "Yes swami" Swami said "Next time don't come alone. Do you understand?"

It is clear the swami has seen with his divine vision the hit squad out there in the dark forest beyond the ashram.

Johnny nodded and came back to his place to sleep. His phone rang and the time was 1:30 AM. He picked up to answer an unknown number. There was silence at the other end and nobody answered. Again he called back and there was no answer. Then he got an idea. Better to end all this charade and be done with it once for all.

Slowly he gathered his belongings and packed his bag. He came out of the ashram and found his footwear out of the very few as the ashram was deserted that day. He started walking towards the bus stop and he knew no bus will run till 6.30 in the morning. That gives B team plenty of time to finish their task and plant any incriminating "evidence". While walking he saw in the dim light of distant mercury vapor lamps, a snake about cross the path. He stood still allowing it to pass. But it seems to have changed its mind and turned back.

In the distance he could sense shadowy figures lurking beyond some bushes and proceeded towards them. At 300 yards from the bushes he stopped knowing that killing range of SLR 7.62 mm round is about the same. In the dim light of the distant mercury vapor lamps, he would make an excellent silhouette which the hit squad could not miss.

Then he shouted "fire"! There was deafening silence from that end and he moved another 100 yards and shouted "hey maa Kay loudey fire" which when loosely translated from Hyderabad Deccani into English means "You mother fuckers, fire".

There was another deafening silence and suddenly a Toyota vehicle zoomed out of darkness towards the highway with great speed. He stood there in silence watching fast disappearing vehicle in the dark.

JR walked to the bus stop, found a bench and lied down waiting for the first bus which usually comes at 6.30 in the morning. No one called him on phone and he had fitful sleep on the cold stone bench the rest of the night. The first bus came at 6; 30 AM in the morning and he reached Hyderabad by 10.00 AM.

Again he went to the ashram next week for B team to complete their unfinished task and again warned by swami not to come alone. Stubbornly he went some more times and finally the swami banished him forever and warned never to come again under any circumstances.

The much eagerly awaited 'encounter' never took place much to the disappointment of Johnny Relevant. Then President visited the city but they seemed to have ignored him not calling in the middle of the night. There was a train derailment, a bank robbery, faction murders in his native district and Trump's daughter too visited the city but the B team ignored him during all those interesting times not bothering to keep an eye on him. The Republic Days and Independence Days also came and went with B team ignoring him altogether.

Earlier, during his visit to Calcutta on his way to Assam, whatever number he called used to get a standard response "West Bengal police" amusing him to no end. But in the last visit to Tarapeeeth, WB police didn't bother him. Which means enlightenment reached them also.

Finally all seem to have got enlightened and understood that Johnny Relevant is a small time crook only and not capable of momentous achievements in their favorite field of terrorism.

But JR never understood till now what made the hit squad come out of their burrows and run for their lives on the day of "Encounter"!

Tag words: Police surveillance, encounter, spirituality third degree treatment. SLR 7.62 and Carbine

Death of a Spy

The sudden demise of Flt Lt Rajesh Kumar aka Swami Prabhupadananda

"I hate Mig21! Thundered Swami Prabhupadananda with fire in his eyes. I said "Well it is a machine of war and it did its job splendidly. And that is the reason Air force is prolonging its life by many upgrades as no suitable replacements were found till now"

He said "you know when the 500 kg bomb is released, nothing survives in a one mile radius. So I was always on lookout for destroying at least one plane n my service."

He said "While on sorties, I hid a bottle of rum in my flying suit and smashed my plane while landing to wreck that aircraft. You can see the cut in my head as I got hit in the impact and my right eye came out of socket and was hanging out" I did see a huge gash on his head and was convinced but could not understand his hatred for MiG 21s.He claimed his father was a Lt Colonel in Maratha Light Infantry and he earned more than his father's salary".

After loss of my job, I was unable to pay EMIs of my flat and the finance company was harassing us. I did a stupid mistake by going for private finance even though I could have easily obtained loan from Government bank. They won't harass defaulters personally especially after recent incidents of suicides of borrowers due to torture by collection agencies and court judgments. So banks, after waiting for several years for defaulters to pay up, will dispose of the property in a public auction. The whole process might take up several years which means rent free accommodation for a long time.

I was hoping to generate money from my unit but it collapsed within few months of starting. I tried my best to dispose of that flat but was unsuccessful in all of my efforts. I would place ads in local papers, take prospective buyers on a visit but nothing came out of all those trips. In fact some of those prospective buyers turned out to be shady characters scouting for a place to come up with some illegal activities.

That was when my daughter found an ad in an astrological magazine in which this Swami had claimed that he is the last resort. After seeing the ad I was intrigued and was surprised by the hubris of that Swami.

We got the address from the astrological magazine, went looking for the Swami and found his place in a remote part of the cantonment. When I knocked on the door, one lean wiry male in his thirties opened the door. We were invited into his place and were seated on the sofa.

Then I noticed a familiar smell coming from the kitchen which I remembered from my childhood but could not fix the cause of the smell. Then I recollected from the days of my childhood spent in slums of railway colony and remembered that same smell from the pots of beef tallow being made from cattle bones of our neighbors. But how do I connect the smell of beef tallow to a supposedly vegetarian Swami? I didn't discuss with that person about his dietary choices due to my taciturn nature and kept my curiosity in check

So here I was meeting him in person. He claimed to be an IAF pilot and left service for the service of humanity. He was dressed in all saffron with a matching turban and looked like an erstwhile Anand Margi. His address was given as a non-descripts two room house on the edge of cantonment and he was practicing astrology, He claimed some friends take care of his needs.

He went on "When I went on bombing missions I used to drop them in the sea so as to not hurt people. You know a 500 Kg bomb destroys very living being in one km radius."

I asked "What about the cameras on board the aircraft?"

He replied "I used to switch off those damn things"

I asked "Were you in 1965 war?" He simply nodded and I went on "One pilot did exactly as you claimed and he was arrested in midflight and brought back to base. After landing the Commanding Officer conducted summary court martial and shot him dead personally in open parade ground. There was talk of some sort of mutiny among the ranks of pilots. Were you aware of that?"

He replied "Really? I was in the eastern front."

Then we raised the subject of sale of my apartment. He said he has some friends who might be interested. They take care of all his needs and shown all the silverware which was gifted by them. Then he proceeded to draw a unique astrological chart likes of which was never seen by me anywhere. In his chart star Arundhati has a prominent place. I wondered why this particular star is not figured in the chart of 27 stars followed in conventional Hindu astrology.

While all this discussion was going on something very strange happened to my daughter and her mother. They collapsed on the sofa and were unable to move. I took leave of the Swami raised them from sofa and got onto our car. After reaching home they reached straight to the bed and flopped down. They fell asleep for twelve hours nonstop much to my surprise. It was as if they were under the possession of some demonic spirit. I wondered at the mystery of it all.

Next time I went alone to him and was told to make offerings to the Goddess at temple at Mushirabad. I was told to buy many types of fruits for offering which I complied. We visited that temple and he asked me recite the Gayatri mantra which he himself could not recite. As the same was being played on the PA system and I recited the mantra. I was intrigued by the Swami and decided to unravel the secret of this god man. But that has to wait for some time as my oracle will not be available until the next Friday. Our oracle is an old lady and answers any query on Friday after 3'o clock only. I decided to meet her next Friday.

I met that person many times to pursue the sale of my apartment but he was evasive and vaguely promised to meet some of his friends who finance his expenses. Once I along with another friend of his had lunch at his place.

I invited the Swami for dinner at my home out of courtesy. He claimed to have crossed into Nepal by foot and travelling abroad in an oil tanker. He claimed to have mastered the art of multiplying currency notes. I was left clueless and wondered how he pulls off such a feat. While dining small talk turned around his exploits in the IAF. I asked him about his war experiences and he claimed he was in the eastern front in 1971 war. I asked whether he was one of the volunteers who were prepared for the Kamikaze attacks on the US 7th fleet Aircraft Carrier, Enterprise. He replied he was not aware of any such group. Then after dinner he went to the wash basin for washing hands. My wife also went there to hand over the towel. I observed him whispering something to my wife. Then I went by car to drop him off at his home and returned about an hour later. I enquired my wife about the secret he whispered and she was silent.

Friday came and I went to our oracle at the ashram. There were not many people on that day and my turn came quickly. As soon I sat in front of her she said "You dined with the devil."

She continued, "His name is the Arabic version of Joseph. He is a traitor and worships the devil. Drink this water and you will be saved." She got a tumbler of water dipped her ring finger of right hand and closed her eyes for some time. I was given the water for drinking which I gulped down. After reaching home I rushed straight to the toilet and had a catharsis. Much purgation followed in the next two days.

After two days I again enquired my wife about the secret whisper of the swami. She asked me "Do you really wish to know?" I said "Yes" "He whispered at the wash basin that you are an old man and cannot satisfy me in bed. He is willing to do the needful." Said my wife. I smiled at her answer and decided to pay one last visit to the god man.

Next day I paid him a visit and said" You are not a pilot and not even a Hindu. Your game is up. I know the reason for your camping at the cantonment. One phone call and you will regret you were ever born"

He said rather boastfully "All the cops in the neighborhood know me." After speaking to that Swami, I returned to my place.

We had a land line newly installed and it was more of a novelty than a utility. Some random phone calls started to that phone enquiring about one Kishore's printing press. The phone would start ringing in the middle of the night for one Kishore. I checked the telephone directory and there was no printing press in our locality.

Before the advent of mobile phones land lines were only means of communications and also of surveillance. To monitor any phone, it is called from the control room which makes the subject phone "hot." Whoever calls the "hot' phone is immediately known to the control room.

We had no one to call except my senile old grandmother at our village. I did not wish to make her head of a sleeper cell or anybody else and so altogether avoided the use of that phone.

Then the phone became silent with no pesky calls in the middle of the night.

After nearly one year I read a newspaper column about death of one astrologer due to overdrinking. I knew better as he was a dedicated soldier of the secret cause and had no vices like drinking or smoking.

Ps: In one dream, he was seen sitting in a front row of a theater or some such place without the uniform of Anand Margi. I also was in the same row and he was glaring at me as though I snitched on him. There was no need for snitching as our intelligence agencies were very capable. He was sticking like a sore thumb with that outlandish garb of an Anand Margi. My guess is he took cyanide to avoid visiting the "nail factory".

Tag words: IAF, MiG 21, Astrology, Arundhati star.

Johnny Relevant and KGF

Rage of The divine feminine

After several years of slogging, finally we managed to buy a flat in a gated community. It was a great buy with 24 hours security and full CCTV coverage. So safety and security was assured more over no howling dogs in the middle of the night to disturb our sleep. This was a greatest blessing as dogs are very territorial and any stray entering the premises tend to settle down and claim ownership. Better not befriend any stray dog and give it shelter: the security were given strict instruction, so peace is maintained. Once any dog is allowed to settle in and if any other dog starts sniffing around, the first one will fight tooth and nail literally to defend his turf. As dogs love fighting all other passing strays too join the battle creating massive ruckus. So the security at the gate were given strict instructions not to allow any stray dog to walk in and told to shoo away stray dogs to maintain peace and also ensure safety of small kids in the community.

Ours is a two room flat whereas my neighbor's is a single bed room one. We found a senior citizen residing alone in the flat and could not meet ever since we purchased our flat two months back. I decided to meet him someday to know him better.

So on a Sunday morning, I went and knocked on my neighbor's door. A grey haired gentleman opened the door and I introduced myself as his neighbor. As he let me in, I noticed the place covered with books and a work table with electronic tools and some components strewn around. There was a laptop on which he was browsing something. I gathered that he is a senior engineer with his only daughter married and settled in the US. Her mother also gone with her daughter leaving this gentleman alone. That is all I could gather about him so far. He seemed to love his loneliness with doing all his chores by himself with a maid coming in the evening for washing dishes and other tasks. He does his cooking himself and visits the supermarket now and then for provisions.

As I settled down in the sofa, I introduced myself' Sir, I am your neighbor and have moved in two months ago. You seem to be living alone in this place. In case you need anything, please let us know."

He said" I am at peace with myself being alone." "What about your family?" I asked.

He replied "I have one daughter living in US along with her mom." And continued "now that I am alone at peace with myself"

"You see my wife is a bitch and has a mind of her own. Doesn't bother about anyone. I was shocked and horrified at his outburst "You seem to be very temperamental sir." He replied "Due to that quarrelsome bitch, we have to shift residence many times."

He replied "My wife used to sweep our garbage towards our neighbor's door and no amount of counselling would make her change her ways. To maintain peace, I engaged a maid. My wife would throw garbage from our third floor flat unmindful of consequences. So I would collect garbage and go to the dump before she wakes up. Now that she is with her daughter in the US, I am at peace. My daughter has a blind spot for her mom and would fight with anyone in her support. Now that both are away from my sight, I am feeling blessed in my solitude.

I said "You don't seem to be keen to visit your people in US"

'No not at all. I am at peace all alone here. My only fear is my daughter and her mom getting into trouble with the law in the US. You see her mom is a pig and likes quarrelling with everyone whether it is for a seat in a bus or train. Here in our country, our people have a forgiving attitude towards the elderly women. If she continues with the attitude there, I have this recurring nightmare of a burly cop strangling her dainty neck with a chokehold and killing her. Then as usual her doting daughter joins the fight and also goes to prison with no repercussions for the cops. You see the cops in US enjoy blanket immunity and as I watch the happenings on TV I am terrified for them. The cops don't seem to be gender sensitive.

They treat everyone same whether a burly black male or a frail Hindu woman. So every morning I call them to assure myself that all is well."

He went on "You see I am a man of peace and avoid confrontation at all costs. Yet people seem to hate me for no reason. Perhaps it has something to do with my horoscope. So I keep to myself not to get into any trouble. Even the maid I engaged was taken after thorough vetting"

I said "For any help, you please call me."

He looked at me and said" My needs are very limited and the maid looks after me really well. Apart from my books and TV I really don't need much, in case I need any component for my experimental circuits, I hire auto to go to the city to get them. My hobby is electronics and go on designing circuits or follow other publications".

I came to know that he is a B E, MBA and was more curious about his accomplishments. So I asked" Sir, you seemed to highly qualified but still leading a modest life. Would you care to share your achievements?"

He went in to get some tea and some biscuits and place the tray before us.

He said "Like I said earlier, I avoid confrontation and have no prejudice towards anyone. I liked the famous motto 'love towards all, hatred towards none. But many times I was thrust into confrontation without any choice."

I asked "Sir, would you like to share your experience

'During my long innings in private sector, I was forced to meet many types of persons and certain incidents stand out as extraordinary. You might say almost paranormal. I was forced to face certain group of people and one group from coastal Andhra need to be mentioned in particular".

Nibbling at the biscuits and sipping the tea I said "Please continue your story as I am more than curious"

He said "there were three major incidents in my life where I was pitted against a particular group unwittingly in which I had no choice.'

"Let me start from the beginning. After getting my engineering degree, I relocated to Hyderabad with my wife looking for a job. My class mate advised me to start looking for job around Kushaiguda where a cluster of electronic industries were located. I applied and got a job in a small company making signaling equipment for railways. One day as I was returning from the canteen after lunch, I saw a wanted poster and found a neighboring company called Advance Data Systems looking for fresh graduates. The salary offered was one thousand rupees per month which was three times my present salary.

"I applied and was called for an interview. The MD, his name was Prasad interviewed me and I think I did very well. As the interview was ending, he asked me about my caste. I was shocked and wondered how someone's caste determines suitability for the job. Those days I was enamored with Jesus and his teachings and considered myself as Christian."

I said "Are you not a Christian anymore?" He replied "more on that later."

"So when I blurted out my reply, his face turned dark and I didn't know the reason. My ordeal started from the next day as I was summoned to the MD's cabin. He threw a pile of Hewlett Packard manuals at me and told me to design a 5 volt 5 amps power supply. In those days power supplies were exclusively linear and the modern-day converters were yet to appear on the horizon. I collected white papers and got down to work. I had drawn a presentable circuit diagram and went to his cabin. That Prasad, MD took one look at my paper and threw it at my face. I was appalled and went back to work and came up with another design. It also got the same response. Out of four newcomers I alone was singled out for humiliation. He was determined to find some fault in my work and going through my papers with a fine tooth comb. It went on for three days and on the fourth day I realised that this person is forcing me to quit on my own. So on the fourth day I walked into his cabin and told him that I am leaving. His face remained expressionless. I left the factory and reached home

"As I came home depressed my dim wit wife said that an old woman had visited our place and told her that I should not be too frank in my dealings with others in the work place. She also told us to visit Tuljapur to get the blessings of the Goddess.

"We didn't have money and also didn't how to reach that place. So I left it at that and went back to Karnataka state and after many struggles got a job in a college. But within one year I relocated to Hyderabad as I got a job as assistant engineer in HAL. There as I was handling test equipment, I saw the power supplies made by the same Advance Data Systems lying as scrap. When enquired about them I was told that spares are not available for servicing those power supplies as the company had closed down.

"Deep down I realized someone above taken vengeance. Later I came to know that in those parts of AP, a Christian is synonymous Dalit. Yet I could not understand the pathological hatred of one community towards Dalit's without any reason.

He continued" I was in an executive position in a Government department as a fresh entrant. In those days MBA was all the rage and I thought that acquiring that degree would help me in my career. I thought of joining after getting my MBA. So I quit my government job to pursue that degree and after slogging for two years and many lakhs rupees, decided to approach my parent department. To my utter shock. The doors were closed and I was left jobless. I was on the lookout for a job, any job. I got some teaching jobs in some colleges but as attendance was falling my department was closed. So again I was on the road.

"He said "I am not sure but there were two more companies that bit the dust and I sensed a pattern. In fact I became a grim reaper for two more such companies"

"But the second one was even more shocking in its ruthlessness in treating the staff.

"In our fight for survival, we ended up again in a residential junior college in the middle of the rice bowl of Karnataka state. My daughter was also offered a job as science teacher and me as maths teacher. We were given a quarter, one of the two in a desolate stretch of road on the highway. There were no inhabitations nearby except some labour huts on the other side of the highway for accommodating the coolies working in the rice mill. The rice mill also was owned by the same Giri Prasad who was running the residential school.

"It seems this Prasad maintained a harem in Bangalore and was always on the lookout for fresh faces among the new teachers of his school. Looks like his eyes fell on my daughter and was waiting for a chance. Once I went to Hyderabad for my daughter's school certificate and the guy next door who was a spy and pimp for that Prasad passed on the message. As I applied for leave that Prasad knew of my movements and got his team ready.

"In the middle of the night, one group claiming to be students returning from a sports meet, started banging on the door of our house demanding some water. My wife could not understand as why those students, instead of going to the hostel have come to my place demanding water. She sensed something fishy but showed a remarkable presence of mind and never opened the door in spite of repeated banging. Even the widow was not opened to look at those "students". After what seemed an eternity the next door opened as the commotion seemed to have attracted attention of the passing traffic and someone came to enquire.

"Finally the neighbor came out and admonished the "students" for coming to the wrong place and told them to go back to the hostel for whatever they want.

"I returned to my quarter the next day and this incident was narrated by my wife. I didn't understand anything at all of that entire episode. Then I forgot all about it. Just as we got our salary, we were told that all the staff are terminated with immediate effect without assigning any reason. Within three months of joining we were told to quit.

I asked the old man "did you not suspect anything fishy in the mass termination of all the staff?'

He said "Hiring and firing is the prerogative of the proprietor of any private firm. Since that school was run as a private institution, without any Government funding, they are not accountable to anybody." Then all the thirty teaching staff who migrated to that god forsaken place were told to quit after collecting their salaries.

"We too were told to vacate the school quarters within one week and we were stranded in that god forsaken place and it was called Saluvanchi mara.

"Later a medium told me in a train journey that that Giri Prasad sensing my absence sent his loyal gang of coolies to bodily lift my daughter and bring to his guest house. After his purpose is served he was ready to throw some bundle of notes towards me. He expected no retribution: Such is the arrogance of that person. Since his plan didn't work out he wanted to sack us; as sacking the two of us alone would arouse suspicion, and so he dismissed the whole staff to avoid it.

I was too shocked to respond to that revelation.

"Later I came to know that his rice mill was sold and all his ill-gotten wealth by dealing in fake currency has vanished except the residential school. But I too have my mission waiting to be accomplished and I will someday find time to go and complete it. God had done his part and I too have to complete my part. I usually ignore minor daily insults but for this one I am keeping my secret powerful weapon for use against that bastard.

What about the third case?" I asked him.

"I will be right back" he said and went inside to get some coffee.

He returned with two mugs of coffee and some biscuits in a tray, placed on the small table.

He began "Before proceeding to the third case which is terrifying in its retribution, I would like to continue our story in the rice bowl of Karnataka.

He asked "Do you believe that a project costing Rupees 550 crores or 5.5 Billion Rupees can be destroyed for a mere 14 thousand rupees job? "

I replied "No sir, I can't believe it"

The old man said "No one believes it including myself"

Anyway we were told to vacate the quarter soon after receiving our salary and we had nowhere to go. We begged that Giri Prasad to give us some time, and after repeated pleadings, were granted one week extension. That grace time we used to find some job in that god forsaken place and made friends with an accountant of another rice mill. I was given a job as junior accountant with a salary of Rs 4000/pm which was reduced to 2000 for some minor infraction. That mill had also came up during the golden days of that team and I was told by one poor cousin of Prasad, they were all in fake currency circulation racket thick as thieves.

"It was the harvest season and there were hundreds of truckloads of paddy entering the premises every day. I sensed great fraud being committed on some dim witted farmers. If a farmer sends 36 truckloads of paddy, they will be counted as 34 literally stealing two truckloads. Another trick was in the accounting books. If a farmer takes a loan of three lakhs rupees, it is entered as three lakhs fifty thousand. In some more gullible farmer's account two lakhs will be entered as three lakhs overwriting digit two as three.

"As told earlier, I took leave for one day and we all went to our native place but I believe I told the owner that we are going to Hyderabad. After we returned to that mill, I was told to quit as I lied about going to Hyderabad but went to our place instead. After much pleading by my accountant friend, I was told to join but at half the salary of two thousand that also if I confess my sin of lying. I decided it is not worth but try my luck in a bigger and more industrially advanced town of Bellary.

"One sethji on coming to know of our plight got me a job of foreman in a small unit of six workers.

The businessman running it was equally ruthless with everyone. There were no favourites. I had to keep standing for twelve hours at a stretch. From there we came to the third and most brutal part of my life.

"He paused and said "I must mention the role of Pastor Stephen Paul in getting us a blessing. As he came to Karnataka state for a three day anointing service, I was prompted by my daughter to attend his service. I did and met him in person. He gifted one of his shirts and told me to get baptized on the last day of the prayer meeting. I did as told and got a job in a highway project as technical assistant at a salary of Rupees 14,000pm.

"I left that place in Karnataka and joined that company in Adilabad. It was located 20 km from the Adilabad town and we were provided accommodation in readymade steel shelters. I too got mine and after joining, went back to get my daughter and her mom. Adilabad is known for extreme climate; burning heat in summer and freezing cold in winter.

"As we settled into our new environment, I realized the strong presence of one community in the company. All higher level positions were occupied by that community. They were all over the place. One M Tech civil engineer from other community was forced to work as assistant for a diploma candidate and another matric fail was a manager in purchase department. He could not write his own name in English. Any way as we got familiar with that predominantly civil engineering project, I was assigned to the Electric engineering department. My boss was a B Tech with three years of experience by name Prasad.

"Our history of hardships had already reached the camp even before I reached the site. One thing about those people is they hate the poor with limited means. So I was treated as dirt by our department head.

"One day one 15kva diesel generating set had gone bad. So this Prathap called for me and I started inspecting the unit. My expertise is electronics and I had never seen a diesel generating set. I started the engine and ran it at full speed and there was no output voltage on any of the three phases. I increased speed then reduced but the output was still zero. I took apart the front panel, thoroughly inspected and found three huge electrolyte capacitors across the three phases. They seemed to be the weakest link and if one fails, all outputs will be shorted. I presented my diagnosis to that boss and he scoffed at me. He ignored me and called for the service engineer from Hyderabad; he arrived after two days. After testing the set, he also gave the same findings. That was my moment of reckoning as that team doesn't appreciate others skills; their people are supposed to be only genius in the country. No one must be more intelligent than engineers belonging to that community.

"So from that moment on wards I was treated like an untouchable in the company with everyone ignoring me. The icing on the cake was calumny and slander. Rumours were being floated that I am an idiot and dumped on the company by some well-meaning director and am a burden. Salary was being paid regularly and I was told by one adviser to speak to the Project Manager by name, Luvakumar; another cousin of the higher ups in his thirties.

"I hanged on to the job as there was no openings anywhere. One year passed and everyone got a raise except me. I didn't know whom to approach as everyone ignored me. They are an effeminate provincial bunch of peasants sharing gossip and mocking everyone else.

"I took leave of two days to visit my old church in the middle of nowhere near Sindhanur. During the sermon the preacher said "I will remove one eye, one hand and one leg from that gang of three".

"I gathered that the three were the Project Manager, Lava Kumar, Prathap, HOD of electrical department and Vasantha Rao, the illiterate Purchase Manager. I didn't share it with anyone as nobody would believe me.

"One day while overseeing the earthwork, one JCB ran over the foot of that Prathap Kumar. One part of prophesy was fulfilled and I didn't stay back in that company long enough to know about the other two.

I returned to the camp and resumed my non-existent work. Someone advised me to speak to the PM to assign me any work

"So I went and spoke to him for some sort of assignment to discharge my duties. He told me to visit all the generators and update the diesel consumption data. I took a motorcycle and went on visiting all the diesel generators on the 55 kilometers stretch of highway. This went on for some months.

"Meanwhile in the camp, there used to be weekly breakfast meeting in the company office on Saturdays. I also used to attend those meetings like everybody else. One Saturday during the meeting, this PM called me in front everyone and said without any prelude "Will you leave this company or do I kick you out?"

I asked him" What was the provocation"

He said "nothing I could think of" and added "Only our utter helpless state of sticking on to the job in spite of being ignored for several months might have been the reason. One thing that community hates is downtrodden. That caste worships wealth and have-nots do not figure in their scheme of things.

He added "I was flabbergasted at this unexpected outburst of hate but recovered. I said that I am ready to leave as that Lava Kumar really did not give me any choice. It was a question made point blank and I had to answer.

"There was pin drop silence in the conference hall. Me a senior engineer with more than 20 years of experience and this cousin of a rich peasant humiliating in a conference. During my stint in defense industry I found a lacuna in the testing of MiG 27 Avionics, which made me not pass the concerned avionic system. The result was piling up all the systems and stopping production of the MiG 27 fleet. The matter reached Defense Ministry, and the Russian Design bureau rushed their chief designer to India to rewrite the specs. Also I designed many turnkey equipment's to DRDO labs and here one trash of a rustic peasant with barely six years of experience humiliated me in the office in public.

"After this public humiliation, I went back to my quarter and wrote a resignation letter to relieve me immediately by paying all dues of the notice period of three months. After reading my letter that PM got furious and wished to know from the HR about duration of notice period. HR said it is one month and I said it is OK with me. That idiot of a PM doesn't know the basic service rules.

"This Lava Kumar thought it over and said "I will let you know after one month'

"And I resumed my old way of motorcycle riding the entire stretch of 55km and checking the generators.

"Within a week I received a call from HR and told to proceed to Subansiri Hydroelectric project at Assam as head of electrical engineering department.

The Empire struck back for talking back to the brother in law. He didn't give me any chance.

"I never been to that part of country and accepted the shifting. I sent my daughter to college in Warangal and I left for Assam.

"The project site was across Subansiri River which flows from Tibet into Arunachal Pradesh. It is a 2000 Megawatt hydroelectric project. There was no electric grid from the country as northeast was not much developed at that time. The project site as well as the camp were supplied totally by diesel generators from 15kva to 1110kva massive DG sets of Caterpillar Company. There were only three 110kV DGs out of which only two were functional.

"The only plus point was I had an excellent team of highly skilled fifty workers but not so skilled engineers. I was given a quarter and designated as Head of Electrical Engineering Department, only to mock me before kicking out.

He looked at me and said" Is it boring to listen to all my troubles?' I replied, "No sir, please go on, it is really very interesting."

He said, "It won't take long, I am almost done."

"Anyway, the greatest problem in that project was seepage of water: water gushes out from the ground, from the sides of the earthwork and has to be pumped out dry for laying concrete bedding. "No amount pumping is adequate as they were fighting a losing battle with nature. There were no sufficient DG sets to run the water pumps.

"One night as I was sleeping in my bed, I saw a lady fully clothed in regal robes hoverering near the ceiling. She said "You will receive one lakh rupees after three months." I woke up wondering whether it is a dream or a vision. My salary was only Rupees 14000 pm and I was wondering how that prophesy is going to be fulfilled.

"When I took over I was told that one 1010 kva DG of Caterpillar was abandoned in the middle of the river and lying there for the last one year. The output voltage control regulator seemed to have gone bad and they had procured a new one which is not matching.

The AVR is in the part of control loop which senses the output voltage and generates correctional DC voltage to keep the output voltage of the generator within limits; this much theory I know but never seen diesel generator of one megawatt capacity until then

"I studied the both old and new AVRs and noticed that the original one runs on 60 volts two phase, generating correction voltage to the field windings to maintain the output within limits. The new one procured was three phase 160 volts which obviously did not match. Nobody had a clue including the service engineer of Caterpillar Company, a graduate of NIT.

'I took intuitive, got two fully charged batteries, lube oil cans, sufficient diesel and left for the defunct DG dumped on an island of the river by boat. We took all the necessary spares and reached the island. We connected the batteries and went on turning the ignition to start the behemoth. Finally the batteries were drained and we returned to the workshop to return the next day.

"The next day we tried turning the flywheel with a crowbar and connected the batteries. As we turned on the ignition, the beast came out of hibernation and started with a roar. But after running for few seconds, it went off with a warning A8, and displaying 'high voltage' and showing 500 volts.

"I had observed two small potentiometers with heads sticking out from the solid potted module AVR, Automatic Voltage Regulator. When the machine was started again, I turned one 2 mm pot slightly half a turn and the machine stopped with warning 'low voltage 'showing 380 volts and displaying A7 as error code.

"I was jubilant for making the beast start and got its secret to control. When it started again, I turned the pot meter with that small screw driver and brought the voltage to exactly 440volts. I ran the set till the end of shift and the news spread throughout the camp like wildfire.

For the first time in my life I was happy for choosing electronics as elective instead of civil engineering as at that even failed candidates were chosen to work in Almatty project. Electronics was seen as a discipline with no future.

"A crane was quickly brought and the DG was shifted to the dam site. Many dewatering pumps were connected and the mission went on at a brisk pace. The concrete went on raising steadily to the desired level. The DG was put to work and it ran nonstop for 15 days and stopped only for topping up the coolant.

"Meanwhile, at the corporate office, the brother in law of the Project Manager, I think his name was Ramesh was keeping regular tabs on me through his network. It speaks volumes about the professionalism of that company where the Chairman keeps tabs on a lowly paid worker out of vendetta. The office staff started believing that I am the blue eyed boy of the Chairman as he went on enquiring about me. The Chairman of several thousand crores of projects was watching over me; I think you get the drift.

I replied "Why a chairman keeps tabs on a lowly worker?"

He said "The HR person, a colonel, at that site also was curious about it. He would call me into his cabin and enquired about my situation. Military officers are full of dignity and grace; they treat everyone with dignity. But these thugs are from rural feudal background became wealthy by hook or crook. They are not used to be talked back and one must suffer any insults silently which a senior person would not bear.

He continued, "That Project Manager didn't give me any choice and other alternative was being kicked out physically. So I took the only option of quitting on my own which ruffled their feathers. They were mightily offended.

"He said, hear me out. Well as everyone was celebrating the success of the dewatering mission, I was told to report to the Head Office at Hyderabad after exactly three months of working.

"I returned to the camp office at Adilabad and met the old friends. After listening to my story many advised me to go to court about the unfair treatment. But one gentleman by name Subba Rao met me in private and advised me against it. He told me that they belong to a very powerful and closely knit group called KGF and nobody can defeat them in courts or outside. If push comes to shove, they would physically eliminate him.

I believed him convinced about the power of that secretive group called KGF to which Giri, that owner of Residential school in Karnataka also belongs. The brazen attempt to kidnap my daughter to rape unmindful of the consequences is a testament to the clout and power of that group.

"So I returned to the head office and was told to submit my report which I did. Then I was told to resign which after some hesitation, I submitted the resignation. I was told to collect my dues after two days. I went back to Warangal and returned after two days to collect my check. With three months' salary and provident fund, it all came to exactly one lakh rupees as prophesied three months earlier by the lady in white.

"With that money we made reservations to Chennai and then to Vailankanni as I was told that the Lady in White was Mother Mary and she called me to visit her shrine.

"I had never been to that place and we got church accommodation without any hassles. I sensed some power in that place. There seems to be a vortex of space and time in that place.

"After supper we went to bed. I had a dream of being pinned down to a dry lake bed with no way of escape. Then someone opened some sort of flood gates and a huge tidal wave rushed towards me but somehow I broke the chains Houdini like and I was standing on the banks of the reservoir.

"Then I heard a voice "I have destroyed AP06"

' I have destroyed AP06'.

"AP06 is the project designation given to the stretch of 55km four lane highway project run by that same Lava Kumar It is a 550 crores rupee project and no one believes my story and so I didn't bother to share it. But I heard news of trouble with toll booths and they were fighting it out in Supreme Court.

I asked "What happened to your family?"

He replied "With the job gone, I had to pull her out of college and we were back in Hyderabad looking for jobs. My daughter suffered a nervous breakdown as she has to discontinue her college. Later I got into an engineering college as foreman, then as a techno commercial manager in a private firm catering to defense labs. My daughter did her graduation through Open University and got married to an NRI. Now she is in the US and sends me money for my rent and monthly expenses.

I asked "What about the gang of three?"

He replied" I searched FB for that Luvakumar and found his profile picture. His both eyes were intact and I often wondered about that prophesy. Only Prathap had his foot crushed by a JCB which I witnessed in person right in my presence in AP06.

"God said 'I will kill them all' in one sermon and often I wonder whether it is a physical or professional death He had in His mind. It might be a metaphorical death. Anyway I have no contact with them and Lava Kumar profile was missing in FB nowadays. May be he is dead"

I was silent for some time with my eyes becoming moist with tears.

He continued" I remained a faithful Christian and was attending a church in Gudihathnoor near our camp. The pastor by name Johnson became my friend and after coming out of that company we settled in Hyderabad again looking for any job.

Then one day I received a call from that pastor Johnson. He said "Jesus visited him and told him to pass on a message to me. I have to pay tithe to the first pastor when I get any income, and that company shall call me back with an offer of double the salary. I got some minor works and after getting paid, paid my tithe to the first pastor, Alex who baptized me. But nothing happened and nobody called me. That failed prophesy was the last nail in the coffin of my faith in Christianity.

"Then I recollected an incident at the time of my baptism. As we were going by our car to the lake for getting dipped as part of the ritual of baptism, a huge snake crossed the road and almost came under our car. Just as the tire was about to run over the snake it suddenly retreated as fast as it came.

Also I remembered an incident in Karnataka state when a young highly gifted preacher from Mysore was praying for me and suddenly there was trembling of the floor. Then the preacher stopped and said "There is a blue green entity with fangs behind you. And it is saying that your prayers are useless and you would hang yourself."

"I was flabbergasted and wondered did not Jesus claim that He is the way and truth. Nobody goes to the Father except through him (Jesus).

"I did study the Bible thoroughly and found that in Numbers, Moses commands his people to look at the Bronze snake and get healed of their afflictions. Looking at might mean to worship the Bronze snake. Later Hezekiah destroys the Bronze snake. I sensed that there might be power struggles between Reptilians goddess and followers of Moses or Christian God of Yahweh.

"What more discovery you found in the Bible"? I asked.

He said" yes I found one particular verse in Old Testament: that is Deuteronomy chapter 32:8 Song of Moses. I will reproduce it now verbatim.

Deuteronomy: 32:8 The Most High assigned nations their lands;

He determined where peoples should live.

He assigned to each nation a god,

But Jacob's descendants he chose for himself.

You highlight that part "He assigned to each nation a god" This particular verse is missing in many Bibles as I seek this verse whenever I visit any church. It looks like there is a deliberate attempt to obliterate traces of all other gods to the exclusion of Yahweh. This led me to more confusion and finally I stopped going to church altogether. The failed prophesy sent to the pastor at Gudihathnoor by Jesus Himself finally made me stop believing in Christianity.

That was the saga of a one ex Christian and I was more shocked than ever about powerlessness of the Gods.

Tag words: Mother Mary, Vailankanni, Luvakumar, AP06, AVR, Caterpillar. Subansiri, Deuteronomy, MiG27. Gudihathnoor, Pastor Johnson.

Narasimha Sashtri Our Class Teacher

Protected by the neighbors

This incident happened in my 7th standard. Narasimha Sashtri was our class teacher and he was a regular comedian. His classes were full of drama and mirth. His rendition of Archimedes principle was a classic comedy. As per his version, after hitting upon the principle of buoyancy while bathing naked in the bathtub, Archimedes ran out from the bath tub in his birthday suit shouting Eureka on the streets of Syracuse. Then the servant followed with his robe followed by his wife with the family dog in tow. As per his version instead of the king, the queen met him first in his birthday suit and ran away into the palace much embarrassed. Then the king appeared later and advised him to get dressed up first and come and meet him in court to explain his findings. Fortunately it was all boys' school with no TV channels to monitor every move trying to catch an unguarded moment. Everything was politically correct in those days.

His rendering of Abhignana Shakuntalam where the famous sage Vishwamitra abandons his penance to frolic with the celestial nymph Menaka was magic to behold. And after begetting Shakuntala, he abandons her to resume his penance. He used to enact the entire story in such a way that would make everyone empathize with the great sage.

As mentioned it was all boys' school and our class teacher had a sister, Geetha also a teacher working in another Government school for girls. She had a colleague from Kadapa in the same school. One day they had a catfight in a staff room and the quarrel lasted several months. Finally it escalated into physical fight with the Headmaster remaining neutral. She carried the tale to her home and our class teacher himself entered the scene. The other teacher used to live alone and she had five brothers back at Kadapa and they were reputed to be factionists.

Narasimha sashtri went to the other teacher's residence and got physical with her. That was when things turned from bad to worse. She warned of dire consequences not only to him but to his entire house hold. Her five brothers in Kadapa were all rich landlords to whom she narrated the whole story over phone. Those days' phones were only landline and it used to take 10 years waiting to get a phone as trenches have to be dug to lay those lines. Only rich people had those phones. Anyway she sent word to our teacher's home to get ready to meet her brothers. On the day of the impending visit of her brothers, she sent word to them through the servant maid to show the same bravery in meeting her brothers.

As the news of her brothers' impending visit came, there was great commotion in our class teacher's home. There was great wailing as all the members were terrified of the attack. The band of brothers were rumored be violent factionists and think nothing of eliminating whole families. There were legendary tales of their ferocity which stuck terror in the hearts of their family members. All that crying and wailing was heard by the neighbors and every one came running to see what it was all about. They expected to see someone sick or dead but all they saw was collective wailing. They asked them the reason and after listening to the news of the impending attack, told them to calm down. "Leave it to us and we will handle them." the neighbors assured them. Still all the family members were shivering with terror.

Around afternoon, a black Ambassador came to their street and five burly males with moustaches got down. As they started enquiring about the address of our class teacher, the neighbors came out one by one asked the reason for the enquiry. They said they have come to see the warrior who manhandled their sister. The neighbors were about twenty in number and one of them gave a hit with a stick which shocked the attackers. They were fully armed with hunting sickles and reached into their car to get them out. Then all the neighbors pounced on them, started beating with sticks which made them drop the sickles. All the five of them were beaten with whatever was available, kicked them around and tore their clothes. They got into their car in a hurry and drove off to avoid further beating.

After the black Ambassador drove off, neighbors went in to the family and found every one of them right from old granny to toddler silently huddled in terror. One of the neighbors said "It is all right, they have gone and won't bother you ever. Now get up and make some food for the children." The neighbors knew that they won't accept cooked food from others. Otherwise all the neighbors were ready to send rice, curry and dal to the entire household.

Later it came to be known that the teacher from Kadapa went on transfer to her native place and our Narasimha Sashtri's sister changed her place of work to a different school. But the magic was gone from his teaching and it was a very subdued and solemn Narasimha Sashtri after that incident.

National Integration

Case study of a failed experiment

After i5 years of service, I was selected for a General Management course at head office. While going through the list of participants, I noticed my friend Anil is also attending from Lucknow. But mysteriously the name of his wife Vanajakshi is missing. It was rumored that they have split but it came as no surprise as their backgrounds are totally different. At the time of marriage, their horoscopes were studied in great depth by learned pundits and a auspicious moment was chosen for solemnizing the event. All hailed their marriage as a classic example of national integration. Anil from the drought prone Anathapur district and Vanajakshi from Orthodox Mysore made a contrasting pair.

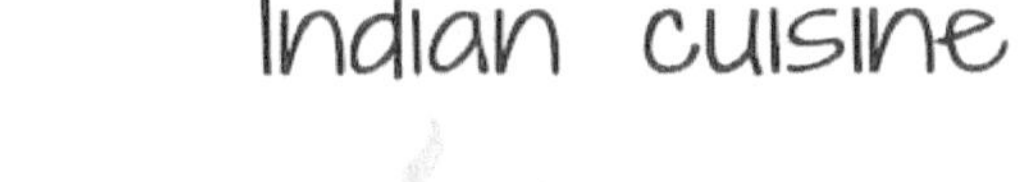

I reached the training center, signed joining report and was allotted a room in the dormitory. In the class I met Anil and after 10 years he has not changed much except some gray hair here and there. Higher management classes were conducted by the faculty from IIMs on contract basis and it was really very helpful. During lunch break, we met in the cafeteria and he gave his room number. I was told to meet him in his room after evening classes were over. Duration of training classes was for 10 days with only break on Sunday and no leaves were allowed except in emergencies.

So I went to his room after the class and was surprised to see him getting ready for a drink. He was a teetotaler in the past and also a non smoker. He offered me a drink but I refused. I wondered what might have caused the split as their horoscopes were studied in great detail by pundits. He was rumored to have a roving eye and an extra marital affair might have been the reason. After taking my seat I said, "So you have hit the bottle. Tell me what happened? Where is Vanni?"

He replied "Do you really wish to know? I said "yes." He said "Curd rice." I exclaimed "What!" and wondered as to how a mundane issue like curd rice might be the reason for split of a love marriage between two educated persons. Thereby hangs a tale.

Anil is from a hardy tribe of people trained to live in most inhospitable desert environment. Their diet used to be millets raised as rain fed crops with occasional rice. They will survive on bajra roti and green chilies but curd is definitely not an essential part of their diet. In fact curd rice causes him to sneeze next day. For Vanajakshi, curd rice is a life and death necessity every day. We used to see him going to the Iyengar's bakery at 10'o clock in the night obviously getting the life saving part of her diet. Without curd rice, she could not sleep and won't allow him to sleep.

I said "Such a simple problem could have been solved with some careful planning." He replied "It is not that simple. They have a practice called 'madi' which is hard to explain. Basically it is a practice to ensure hygiene. The nearest example is something like kosher among Jews. But unlike Judaism which does not prohibit meat eating, this practice is purely vegetarian and seems to have evolved to maintain hygiene. But to him it turned out to be a draconian practice of handling and consuming food."

I replied "You can simply make it at home by adding lemon juice or tamarind to a warm milk." He said "I tried all. Once at supper time she remembered that there is no curd. She was utterly disorganized rushing at last minute to get some missing but important ingredient. I rushed to the only bakery open at that hour to get but she refused to eat because it was not from Iyengar's bakery but Regal Bakery as Iyengar's was closed by 10pm. That night I had hell"

"Well you could have taken the matter into your hands by making it at home yourself as you are good at forward planning." I said.

He replied "Many times I tried making it myself by adding left over curd to a bowl of milk. When she came to know I washed the bowl with the water from the second tap instead of first one which gives madi, that is kosher water, she flew into a rage and refused to have curd rice that day. I had hell trying to sleep that night. I failed to please her kosher demands and was depressed most of the time unable to live up to her exacting standards.

I asked him "how about your favorite foods?' He said it was purely vegetarian all the way as she did not permit even poultry egg at home. It was bland food with no garlic or onions." How I loved the Bombay duck dish my mom used to make. It was pure heaven with bajra roti." He went nostalgic "And the dried shrimp chili powder with a hint of garlic used to make a great accompaniment to the dal rice." I told him "You could have your favorite food in outside hotels." He said "I was free to eat outside now and then but nothing like food made by our people in our hamlet. I used to visit my village during holidays to savor my homely food but it was only temporary reprieve. I gave up non vegetarian food to please her. I could not get appreciation for my 'sacrifice'. It was a worthless sacrifice from my side. So I decided to part ways citing irrevocable difference in a court of law. Now that I am legally divorced and can eat our favorite food like our gunpowder and shrimp chutney as great accompaniments to goat legs curry with rice.

I asked" What Is gunpowder? He went nostalgic and replied it is a mixture of dry red chillies, garlic and dry grated coconut with salt all pounded to a fine mixture. More chilly makes it more appetizing and it explodes on your tongue. That is why it is called gunpowder. We don't need cooling agents like curd to subdue the fire."

"Why did you not marry again?" He laughed "I do not wish take a second risk. You know I am approaching forty and do not wish to open a can of worms by marrying a younger woman at this age.

I said "Your story is hard to believe. There must be something else."

After some time he replied "You know the pros we engaged from Budhwarpet in our room?" I replied "I would rather forget it."

He was reminding me of that incident during our college days. We engaged a prostitute from Budhwarpet and were having a nice time taking turns. After second session, she started shrieking and demanded to be let out terrified of being raped to death. As her shrieks were attracting attention of neighbors, we let her go her through back door paying her 25 rupees in small change. The neighbors knocked on our door and found nothing suspicious. It was a close call and we decided never to take such risk again. We got off by the skin off our teeth.

They were pre AIDS days and any disease like Cancroid, Syphilis or Gonorrhea were promptly treated by our VD Doctor Hegde. AIDS was yet to appear on the horizon and life was simpler.

I asked "what is the point of all this?

He replied "Just for old times' sake.

"Well what I learned is compatibility is the most important element in married life. You see great scientists getting along fine with dim wit wives. It is all in compatibility. You don't need someone to discuss Kafka in the bed room to have a great married life. I studied Chinese Zodiac system which predicts accurately compatibility depending on animal signs. As per that chart the compatibility between us was only 40 percent. Any score below 50 is to be avoided. You see I have prepared a compatibility chart to choose any prospective bride and I am waiting. May be I may meet someone with a compatibility score of 90."

With heavy heart I said "I wish you meet someone with a score of 100 percent soon."

As I was returning to my room, I recollected the words of a famous writer that there are two types of terrorism in an average household. One perpetuated by men in the bedroom and the other one by females in the kitchen.

And I reached my room feeling sad at the failed experiment of National Integration.

Tag words: National integration, divorce, compatibility, Chinese astrology.

The First Kill of LCA

Height of women empowerment

It was 630 in the morning and my newly installed landline phone went on ringing. It was a novelty in those days without the fancy features like called ID and such things. That was my friend Subramanian from Marketing at the other end. He is known for practical jokes. He said "Hey our LCA has scored a hit" I was flabbergasted and shouted into phone "What did a war start somewhere?" There was no reply as Subbu cut the phone

I was left wondering about his cryptic message. Did our LCA beat Chinese Long Dong in dogfights over icy wastes of Tibet? Or their clones in Pakistan? Or the much feared American F16 or F35 over Pakistan? I was full of such doubts as I prepared to the much dreaded monthly review meeting.

I was grumpy that morning with not much sleep with our own mongrel in residence picking up fights with passing strays and the racket didn't help

my sleep at all. On top of that today's is the day of monthly production review meeting chaired by our own formidable General Manager, Colonel Kaliandasany. Full bird Colonel as they say in Hollywood movies.

He is reputed to have an elephantine memory and none can bluff his way out of tight spots. He remembers whatever one commits in a meeting even six months ago. If anyone underestimates him as he is a mechanical engineer running a defense electronic industry he has another think coming?

The other day during visit to the Airborne Radar Division, full power test was going on and for some unknown reason everyone on the shop floor was feeling uncomfortable. Then the GM walks in with all his entourage and after observing for some time says "Something seems to be missing". Everyone was getting cooked in a huge microwave oven and feeling hot.

One technician sheepishly connected the missing antenna load resistor and everything seems to be ok. It should be credited to the designers of that power amplifier that with all that reverse power with no load did not burn the power amplifier.

We reached the conference hall and took our seats. Review started with VHF Communication division. "What is the status of VHF com receivers? GM queried the chief manager. "Sir the front end is being held up by QC sir". "May I know the reason" GM asked. QC manager replied that the module is not meeting the minimum gain requirement of 60dB as per specification and so we cannot pass them. It is generating a gain of only 40 Db. Godbole, also nicknamed The Artful Dodger, the Inventory control manager spearheading Indigenization drive, chipped in "Sir as part of indigenous drive we procured same type of transistors BEL 3N200 from indigenous sources. It met all the performance parameters as per specs and so we released to shop for production after passing through Inwards Goods Inspection... The item not meeting specs in production sets is news to me" GM asked "What is the alternative now" Godbole replied that we have to revert back to the original supplier and use the component from RCA.GM asked "How many per set" Godbole replied "Four transistors for each set and we procured 100 no's for 25 sets. We have to send all the modules for rework to replace the units." What is the lead time" GM asked. Godbole replied "Three weeks at the latest" GM kept silent for some time and was thinking of the explanation to be submitted to the Head Office as he had already committed delivery of 25 units by end of that month.

That is the end of indigenous drive launched by Godbole, The Artful Dodger.

Then there is Kotineni Sambasivarao popularly known as KSR' Chief Manager from System Audit taking notes. He is from Vijayawada and a crusader for eliminating SCs from the face of the earth. The higher ups didn't understand his animosity towards dalits. One engineer from SC community was posted in Radar division under his charge and he made that person's life hell by harassing, micromanaging and determined to throw him out. So he wrote adverse remarks on that engineer and inadvertently the ACR passed all the three levels of review and signed by the GM himself. Nobody noticed the adverse recommendation for extending the probation. So his probation was extended.

One day the probationer went up the roof of five floors and jumped to the ground in a clear case of suicide. As soon his body hit the ground his head split open and he died on the spot. The security staff rushed to the roof of fifth floor and found a note clearly mentioning KSR as responsible for taking that extreme step. The vigilance chief got hold of that note and kept it hidden from everyone except the GM. The GM kept it a secret and put up a story that the engineer went to the Radar antenna for making some adjustments but slipped and fell. But the GM sent a confidential note to Head Quarters and was told to pull out that KSR from active production roles and be shunted out of shop floor. Had the reality leaked out, the SC commission would have come down like a ton of bricks and the stink would have reached the Parliament itself. Many heads would have rolled out.

KSR was given a cabin with one assistant to lord over for sending and receiving correspondence to Head Quarters.

Next was the turn of IFF LCA from R&D division. The shop manager claimed that all the 50 units are pending with QC. The concerned DGM replied that QC is holding version 5 drawings whereas Designs has launched version 7 to the Engineering Dept. "There is utter chaos sir, we do not know which version to use for inspection" The GM smiled and said to himself "Trust the civilians to mess up anything. "He said impatiently to the DGM Designs "Please sort it by the end of the day and keep me posted."

Then came the turn of Army project- Tank Gear Box Controller. "What is the position of this item?" GM queried. QC manager replied "Sir, Army people are not coming for inspection as the modified drawings of the neoprene gasket has not reached them. Marketing claims they have sent amendments but not received by COD Agra." GM demanded to see the dispatch details and was promptly provided. In the mailing list it was sent to Air HQ but not to COD Agra.GM became furious and asked the Marketing DGM "What has Air force got to do with Vijayanta tank? Send the amendment to COD Agra and get extension of delivery period by tomorrow." Same case with naval version of IFF transponder where delivery date has expired and Amended DD was sent to Air HQ instead of Naval HQ and the Marketing Manager got some tongue lashing from GM.

While all this was going on no one mentioned of any air battles or skirmishes anywhere. The GM was not given to small talk apart from the business on hand alone. I expected to listen to the exploits of our LCA in distant lands and every country queuing up to buy our own LCA. I may not be a genius but they may need services of nuts and bolts counter like me. But sadly no one mentioned about any skirmishes. I was dreaming of nude beaches and belly dancers.

Review over and I was relieved for we escaped any reprimand as I went fully prepared. I gave strict instructions to my assistant Raju not to contradict me but discreetly send some slip in case of any mistake from my end.

It was lunch time and we all trooped back to the canteen. Subramanian was holding forth with full gusto at a distant table. After lunch we used to gather at the favorite tree at the rear entrance for small talk before dispersing to our work spots.

As soon I met I shot the question uppermost in my mind "What is the brouhaha about LCA." He said "Relax it is about our own Aruna." I asked "Whatever happened to her." Aruna was from R&D department and was working on Mission Computer of LCA.

Aruna was a short lady and has a combative attitude towards one and all. General Managers dreaded to cross her paths as they are terrified of her combative attitude, her mastery over MIL standards, and hence the nickname LCA, Light Combative Aruna. Then Subramanian filled in the details.

The long and short of it is, she got married to another engineer in an arranged match. He was working in a ceiling fan industry. Aruna graduated from NIT with honors whereas husband passed out from a Rural Engineering college. He is working in a nuts and bolts industry whereas she is working on Mission Computer of LCA no less and so naturally she is superior to him in all respects. So she felt she need not cook, wash his clothes or sleep with him as it is below her station in life. She hated him and all his family members. Fights were raging in her household over trivial issues and finally she used the dreaded Section 498A of India Penal Code, the ultimate weapon of disgruntled and vengeful wives. Her husband and in-laws including his grand ma were arrested and landed in prison. After spending one month in jail, they were released on bail and her husband promptly hanged himself inside the house.

That is the tale of first kill of LCA even before joining squadron service.

Tag words: Mission computer, LCA

The Monk with AIDS

A pastor's grim battle with celibacy

Pastor Prasanna Kumar was an extremely worried man. The collections in church were barely sufficient to pay for the electricity bill to feed him and his assistant. Though he could not blame it on the miserliness of the church members, he knew they were a poor lot and barely surviving with nothing to spare in the form of tithes. He never demanded tithes in his church being aware of the precarious situation of his sheep. Sometimes they offer their local produce of rice and vegetables which he badly needed in view of his precarious situation.

The past months were extremely taxing first with one week of fasting prayer for the marriage of Lalitha followed by another week of fasting prayer for employment of Raghu. And some more fasting prayers followed. Then came Lent with the mandatory fasting for 40 days.

His health was going down with all these fasting and he was feeling weak. Then a new problem came up.

For the last two weeks or so a thick liquid was oozing out of his organ and he was terrified about it. He was a diehard celibate and in spite of all the temptation was grimly holding on to his celibacy. Particularly that girl Shyamala who makes her pallu slip during prayers whether by design or by mistake, he is not sure. And she sits in the church such a way that she exposes her side view in all its glory as if she is taunting him. He had great trouble in averting his gaze from her during prayers. There are many more distractions with other females so that he stopped praying by placing his hand on anybody's head.

As the symptoms were not subsiding, he wanted to seek medical help. With his precarious financial situation he could not afford treatment at a private hospital. So he took a bus to the town and went to the district medical center seeking appointment with Dr Ranga Rao MBBS MD Frcs (Lond), the Chief Medical Officer. There was a long queue and his turn came after waiting for half an hour. He explained his medical condition to the doctor who without even looking up at him told to go to ward no 16.

Off he went to ward no 16 and was shocked. His world came crashing down. It was the HIV ward! How did he get it? He had not taken any injections or blood transfusions even in the distant past. The last known sexual encounter was twenty years ago when he had oral sex in an unguarded moment. He confessed to it several times at Vailankanni also in Retreat at Chalakudi in Kerala.

He was told his sins were forgiven, but why this calamity visiting him now? Is God punishing him for his secret sin now? His spiritual quest took him to Divine Retreat Center at Chalakudi near Ernakulum for one week of prayer and sermons. Accommodation and boarding was provided at a nominal cost for one week residential program. Something extraordinary happened at Chalakudi Retreat.

In one session, a preacher said to the assembly in general without pointing at anyone. "Remember that night when you were stopped on your way to the hostel by two cops. Who do you think came to your rescue that night?"

He was stunned as this incident happened to him thirty years ago while in studying for degree in college. He was returning to his hostel by walk after a rendezvous in a slum. As he turned into the main road, two beat cops were at some distance behind him, blew their whistles shouting at him to stop. His first instinct was to run but he stood his ground. The cops approached him and asked "Where are you coming from?" He replied that he was coming from his friend's room at the medical college hostel. Then they let him go without further questioning. He was surprised at the outcome as he expected to be grilled and taken to the police station for further questioning. That would have exposed his lie and after that he would have left the college in utter shame. He was amazed at the power and love of God who came to his rescue even without asking Him.

In one sermon the preacher said "Remember the heart break in your college days." He was referring to the loss of his only love that he loved madly. Every day he would always hang around her home to catch a glimpse of his angel. Then she went away to study medicine and he went away to a different city. But he was sowing wild oats on the side in secret. The spirit was willing but the flesh was weak. To his utter shock, she got married to her class mate and left for US. Jesus consoled him but surprisingly He did not judge him.

Prasanna Kumar understood the power of sin which separated him from his loved one. Yes sin is real and not to be bandied about in a casual way. He prayed to God, "Lord, I deserve this pain and I am solely responsible for losing her. She deserves a better person than me a, philandering no good bastard." Yes, sin is real and it also made him a better person.

Then he came back to the present crisis. What if the laity comes to know about his medical condition? That would definitely close his church and end his service to God. And the resulting scandal will add to the ongoing campaign of vilification of Christianity. Does the gestation period of AIDS extend to 20 years? It seems God did not really forgiven his secret sins but only waiting for the right time to punish with this dreaded disease After all He is known to be a vengeful God and the retribution shall be swift when He acts.

He came back to his village much depressed and was seeking answers to his predicament. Then he saw a quack named Basava Raj RMP (Electro homeopathy) whatever it means. He had only 10 rupees with him but decided to meet the quack any way. He went in as the "doctor" was alone. He explained his condition and was taken to the examination table. After examining the relevant part, he wrote Becozinc six capsules as the prescription. The fee was 30 rupees which our pastor did not have with him. The "doctor" told him "It is all right, you pay whenever you can."

He purchased six capsules with the ten rupees he had with him and taken one after lunch. Next day morning there was less discharge but to be on safer side he continued the treatment all six days. The pastor's ordeal came to an end with just six capsules of Becozinc. Had he seen a specialist instead of a quack in the village, the outcome would have been tragic.

After this "miracle" Pastor Prasanna Kumar started praying to God with renewed vigor. His sermons were filled with love faith and mercy of God.

Tag words: Chalakudi, Divine retreat center, Becozinc, HIV,

A Perfect Hate Crime

Karma Boomerang

The time was 10 pm and the place was Nehru bus station in Vijayawada. It was summer and extremely hot even at that time of night. Sashidhar came to that city on official work and finished it by six in the evening. He was waiting for his bus to Bangalore which was supposed to reach the platform by that time. Then as time went on a man came to him accompanied by a girl in her twenties. He asked in an accent of coastal Andhra, "Sir will you kindly look after my daughter, I will go and get some fruits for her." Sashidhar said "Ok" went on looking for his bus.

The bus finally came and parked onto the designated platform. There was no trace of the father of that girl. Passengers went on boarding but still no trace of that gentleman. He glanced sideways at the girl and found her to be dusky but beautiful in a homely sort of way. Time was fast approaching for departure and the conductor calling out to passengers to get in. Just then his phone rang and it was his friend Kumar from Bangalore. "Hi have you boarded the bus?" Sashidhar answered "No I am stuck with a girl and her father has left her with me."

Kumar laughed and said "Don't you believe him. What was his name? Ask that girl." Sashi asked that girl "Where did your father go? What is his name?" She answered "My father's name is Paparao and I don't where is he gone."

Shashi called back and passed on the information to Kumar. Kumar said "Just as I expected. Don't you believe them and get into the bus. So Shashi rushed into the bus and took his seat at the last moment. And as the bus started he was wondering about the whole mystery and dozed off.

The bus reached Bangalore and Shashi reached his room. By that time Kumar has already left for his job. Shashi reported for duty was busy whole day filing reports TA and DA claims. At the end of the day, he returned to room and met Kumar who had returned from his job. He asked "Ok, now enlighten me about the mystery" Kumar started explain about previous day's happenings and his cryptic messages. The gist of the tale was as follows.

One of his batch mates got through GATE and landed a job as Design Trainee in a defense PSU. In the assembly building there was an officer from Maharashtra from Mumbai to be specific. He married a nice girl and was staying in company quarters. The officer named Amit Waghmare was working in the assembly as testing engineer and next door was special projects division.

Paparao was posted in that project in which there is no accountability of workers as there is no record of output being a R&D unit. All the engineers were fresher's from engineering college, lacked administrative skills and were mostly immersed in designs. So our Paparao had a free run punching in and after first lunch go out and look after his business interest in real estate, chit funds selling textiles etc. He used to leisurely saunter in second shift and leave after two hours wandering throughout the factory and punching out at General shift at 5 o'clock He had deep contacts within security department selling defense liquor in black-market.

Life was on a roll with assured salary and incentive for whatever the geeks of his department produced. The incentive scheme is a scam designed to keep workers happy for whatever little output they produce. Salary is for punching in attendance and incentive is for the production which is assured to everyone to present on rolls. Subsidized and tea, coffee are also part of the offering for those hard working workmen.

Anyway life was good for our proxy punching free roaming worker. His only problem was with Waghmare in the next door for he came to know that this fellow being a SC married a Brahmin girl which our Apparao found to be very hard to accept. He had intense hatred for this lowly person who had the audacity to marry above his caste and also seems to be flirting with other females.

Paparao used to seethe with rage whenever this engineer found speaking to other females. Back in his village persons of low caste have to be confined to their own settlements and dare not enter the village where high castes live. Even if someone enters the high caste's living quarters he has to stand outside the gate and deliver the message or consignment. After the lowly person leaves that place it had to be cleaned with water. If that low caste person had to walk in front their gate, they have to go barefoot holding the footwear in their hands. It was rumored Papa Rao's father was the leader in one pogrom where Dalit's hamlets were burnt to ground and some were killed while escaping the inferno.

Waghmare became an obsession to Paparao and he used to hang around Wghmare's quarter in the township burning with hate just by looking at his quarter. He used to hang around officer's quarter well into midnight imagining their romantic moments and seething with rage. A Dalit sleeping with a Brahmin woman used keep him awake all night burning with jealousy. When the security jeep met him on rounds on the streets of officer's quarter, he used to bluff his way claiming to be visiting his boss at his home.

So Paparao was burning with hatred towards this upstart and hatching many plans to fix him in some scam which somehow did not materialize. He planned to hit Waghmare as a low caste bastard but with strong Civil Rights laws he dare not do it.

Not long ago Apparao from his village abused another Dalit by his caste name which brought the Dalit leaders to the factory and the management had a tough time diffusing the situation. After Apparao tendered an unconditional apology, the situation was brought under control. The DGM HR did a fine balancing act to keep the matter concealed without the media getting even a hint of the situation.

So Paparao was thinking of a fool proof plan without exposing himself. Then he hit upon a brilliant idea. There was an archaic practice called Duty Officer followed in defense PSU. All middle ranking officers were put on roster every night acting as head of the institution from evening to day break. The purpose behind this practice was not clear as officers from diverse backgrounds like accounts to R&D were put on roster. The Duty Officer is the defacto head of the unit during night time and solely responsible for any eventuality in the factory and township premises during night time.

The importance of the Duty Officer's responsibility could be understood from the following incident.

One night the sub inspector from the police station next to the gate sauntered in to the factory premises in his civvies around 1130 pm. The lone security guard at the gate did not recognize him and enquired about his identity. This infuriated the cop who felt mightily offended at this imaginary slight and called other police personnel from his police station. The security guard was beaten black and blue in the police station for the temerity to ask about the identity of the SI. Then he was thrown into lockup.

When the Duty Officer came on rounds to check, the post was deserted and the guard was found missing. Upon enquiry, it was found that he was in police lock up for asking the identity of the SI. The Duty Officer promptly contacted Chief Security Officer who called up the General Manager in the middle of the night appraising of the situation. The GM in turn called Governor's office and explained the incident. Governor's office called the DGP of the State and the cop was transferred by next morning. Point is any such untoward happening in night is the sole responsibility of the Duty Officer.

When Waghmare's turn came, Paparao hatched a fool proof plan to implicate him. The plan was to fix him as Duty Officer in sale of scrap in an ingenious way. First a small truck will be allowed for weighing at the weigh bridge for tare weight and after getting the printout a different but larger truck will be loaded with scrap. His friends in security followed his plan and loaded the larger truck with aluminum and copper scrap. It got waved through the first gate and reached the outer gate. Then the guard compared the printout with the truck number and found the registration number to be different. The difference in weight was around 2 tons.

He stopped the truck called, Chief Security officer who in turn called the GM. Waghmare was placed under suspension and was told to attend enquiry next day. When he reached home early morning and broke the news to his wife she was heartbroken. While he went to attend the enquiry she along with her 9 year old son hanged to death in the company quarter.

Waghmare was found guilty of negligence if not complicity and dismissed from service. He went missing and his in-laws came from their place performed last rites after the post mortem and vacated the quarter.

Papa Rao's son became mad and was wandering on the roads. His eldest daughter committed suicide at the in-law's place. He took VRS and went back to his place where he mysteriously became a pauper. To survive he became a pimp to his own younger daughter.

After listening to the tale of hate crime, I was shocked beyond belief about the power of hate. He remembered a Hollywood movie seen long time ago and it was called Blow hot blow cold. It was a Hollywood movie about murder due to sexual jealousy.

Tag words: Duty officer, atrocity act, hate crime,

Train to Lucknow

Memories of good old says

Back in the seventies there were no direct trains to Lucknow from Hyderabad. One has to go to Jhansi and get a connecting train to Lucknow. So when we were told to report to a training centre at Lucknow, we boarded the slowest train, the Dakshin Express at Secunderabad leaving at 1030 in the night. It was a mail train and has to pick up mail all along the wayside stations in a leisurely way.

So we boarded that train and got down at Jhansi around midnight. We were running around the station for the train to Lucknow and someone pointed at a parked dark empty rake. We enquired with the station master about the likely departure time of that train. He was very philosophical and said the train would leave whenever it feels like leaving.

We got in one coach and as it was almost empty, made it to some berths and made ourselves comfortable. Our luggage was kept under the berths and to our horror there was water on the floor. Our luggage was getting wet and we promptly retrieved on to our seats to prevent our luggage with clothes and papers from getting wet. Upon close investigation, we found that the water was coming from the toilet and it is draining out from the missing taps. As the coach very dark we searched for the light switch and found some loose wires hanging from the junction box. We touched two wires at random which made the fans started running but no lights came on. We kept the fans on to make the water on the floor evaporate and settled on our berths in pitch darkness to catch some sleep.

After what seemed to be many hours we sensed the train moving and passengers getting at wayside stations. It was day break and we saw vast expanse of flat fertile land with no trace of any stone or granite. In one wayside station, the train seemed to got into a long break as we sensed a crossing there. we got down from the train for some breakfast as we brushed our teeth on the platform itself. Poories were being made on the platform itself and sold at the rate of ten rupees for a plate of six. For ten rupees it was a hearty breakfast if one gets used to the mustard oil used to cook.

For what seemed to be an eternity the crossing train came and left the station. Our train too started and after few minutes, came to a halt. We were curious about the reason but soon saw a milkman furiously cycling towards the train. He came with the milk cans and the crew of the train also came down with jugs to the platform. The milkman filled the driver and his assistant jugs and they went back to the engine to resume the journey. It was repeated at some more stations and each time the milkmen obliged the crew with generous quantity of milk. The crew in turn stopped for the convenience of the milkmen so their business is not hampered due to punctuality of the railways.

As the journey progressed the coach was getting filled with all types of passengers. On gentleman with moustache sat on my opposite seat with a double barrelled shot gun twirling his moustache all the time.

When it seemed that the train is running at good speed, it came to a screeching halt with sudden application of emergency brakes. People sleeping on upper berths tumbled down on to the floor and the double barrel gun of the moustache gentleman went on with a double blast. As the gun went off there were gaping holes in the roof. If someone travelling on the roof top would have gotten pellets in their bottoms. Since nobody was on the roof top, none got hurt.

We all rushed to see the reason for that calamity and came to know that a cow had settled down on the railway tracks happily chewing cud. The sudden braking had stopped the train just few meters from the animal. The sudden stopping caused many to fall down from their berths.

The crew and some passengers limping after the fall got down and cajoled the animal to leave the tracks and settle down somewhere else. The cow was adamant but after repeated cajoling, got up and sauntered away from the tracks.

The train started moving and came to another wayside station. On passenger was sitting near the window resting his hand the bar of the window. As the train started to leave the station on boy started running towards the train. One passenger standing in the door extended his hand to help him get into the coach. Instead that boy grabbed the hand of the person sitting on the widow side and pulled at his watch. The passenger started shouting but in vain; his watch was gone within seconds. The train gathered speed and nobody could do anything: the thief vanished in the fast receding background.

As the journey progressed, the TTE entered the coach and we didn't like everyone else have any tickets. The booking counter at Jhansi was closed and we boarded without any tickets for the onward journey from that station. More over my friend Trinadha Rao had advised me against buying tickets as none bothers about such niceties.

He told me that in case of any query about tickets, all I have to say "Nahi hai" and there ends the matter. So the TTE came and asked my friend first and he said "Nahi hai" and off he went. It was my turn and I too gave the standard reply and again the TTE went away. It was more of a formality on the part of the TTE rather than collect some revenue for the railways. But I felt bad about the whole issue and decided to buy a ticket at least for the rest of the travel. My South Indian integrity wouldn't let me in peace for the rest of the journey or even the rest of life if I travel ticketless.

So at a station called Unnao, the train halted for a considerable time and off I went looking booking office. I found it but it was closed. I frantically searched some official to inform my plight and found the Station Master on the platform about to wave the green flag to start the train. I asked him about the booking counter, and he replied it was closed. I told him that I would like to buy a ticket to Lucknow. He said 'Where are you coming from" in chaste Hindi.

I said "From Jhansi"

The station master replied that since I have travelled so far without ticket, I better complete the journey in the same way and not bother him with opening the booking office and issue the ticket.

I returned crest fallen and got into my seat. The train gathered speed and soon reached Kanpur. There it halted for ten minutes before resuming the onward journey. As the train left Kanpur station, and picking up speed we heard terrible screams of a female near the toilet. One middle aged lady was screaming in terror and pain as her earlobes were dripping with blood. It seems one teenager got into the coach as bonafide passenger at Kanpur and waiting at the toilet for his prey. As the train picked up speed he pounced on the nearest female having gold ear rings and pulled them with full force so the gold ear rings came out puncturing the ear lobes and leaving bleeding cuts. We looked out of the windows to watch the teenager jump from the running train and vanish in the fading back ground. Her husband rushed to the toilet and consoled her and trying to stop the bleeding with a wet handkerchief.

The coach fell silent and I was too depressed to notice anything till the train reached the destination. There also none demanded to see our tickets and we came out to see our transport waiting for us. We got in full six hours behind schedule and went to our training center.

Tag words: Jhansi, Kanpur, Lucknow, TTE, COW ON THE TRACK.

Venkataswamy, My Grandpa's Cousin

A policeman's friendship

This incident happened during my grand pa's time. Our ancestors were small farmers and landless peasants surviving on the scanty rain fall to grow maize and sorghum. Some of them took to share cropping of rich landlords with the meagre produce of one harvest per year. Rest of the time they worked on rich farmer's fields as laborers.

The village of my ancestor fell on the cross roads of railway network being built on the dusty plains with no particular strategic advantage. A huge loco shed was built by the British for service and maintenance of steam locomotives. Spacious railway quarters were built for the supervisory staff with the remarkable feature of maintaining cool temperature even in mid hot summers. But the British needed working hands for running this huge establishment. They were desperately looking for manual labor and scouted the nearby villages for recruitment.

Our ancestors were terrified at the sight of these huge smoke belching Behemoths. Whenever they travel by these steam run passenger train and get to their destination, they would alight and gawk at the ponderous monster and would look out for hidden elephants inside. They were sure that some mighty beast might be pulling those carriages. They knew only bullock cart as a means of transport and this locomotive was an inscrutable mystery.

Anyway, coming back to our story, the British used to raid our villages to scout for able bodied males to be put to work in the loco shed. On seeing them, my ancestors used to run away to the fields but were soon caught and put to work. They used to be given designation of helpers as they were mostly illiterates. Fitter helper and fitter were the aspiration posts for those recruits. Those with some education used to reach the designation of Charge man.

Matriculates would reach the much coveted level of Foreman with the big bungalow after several years of slogging as charge man.

During the time of this story, my grand pa was fitter in the loco shed. They were thrifty people not given to conspicuous consumption given their low salaries. They used to invest money in chits among themselves and there were not many luxurious goods to hanker. A bicycle or a table radio were much prized possessions. Brass and copper vessels were the signs of wealth which were purchased for storing water carried on pots from railway quarters. Water was supplied to the railway quarters on regular timings and kind hearted railway employees would throw open their back yards for the villagers to collect the water which was carried in copper pots with narrow necks to avoid spillage on the long trips to their homes.

With the chit money, they used to buy gold for the marriages. Land was almost free as one could pitch a thatched hut wherever they could find level land. After a day of hard labour, some of them used to partake country liquor which was cheap and was easily available. Coal used to be pilfered from coal yard for cooking and some youth also were engaged in selling it as a source of income. Once lighted the iron stove would last up to two hours and all cooking would have been done once for all. It was a peaceful idyllic existence with an occasional movie in the tent theatre.

One Sunday after making chicken curry of those birds they reared as additional source of income, my grand pa went to the weekly market for some groceries. There he met his long lost child hood friend and class mate in school, Venkataswamy. His joy knew no bounds after seeing him who also happened to be a distant cousin. He invited him for lunch and got him home.

He served him the best dishes his wife cooked for that day. He introduced to his wife and friends this distant cousin Venkataswamy. They asked him about his job and was told that he was in the police department. They didn't give him much thought and were busy partaking the lavish spread. After sumptuous lunch with some country liquor thrown Venkataswamy was given a warm send off after lunch.

The evening was spent in discussing the family ties with old women contributing their tales of pregnancies and deliveries which were used to mark time in their calendars especially during the local Jathras and such momentous events. Others would gather around homes with radio sets to listen to abridged audio tracks of the popular Telugu movies.

In the evening, everyone was shocked to see a police jeep drive up the street and stop at my grand pas house. One sub inspector of police in uniform followed by the cousin Venkataswamy also in uniform got down from the jeep. Some more cops also joined and not even with a nod entered his poor hut. Venkataswamy showed the SI the suspected loot in the form of big brass vessels and copper water tank. The SI barked "From where you stole all these goods, you criminal bastard"! My grand pa and his wife were shocked but recovered soon.

My grand pa said "I have purchased all these from my own earnings" and proceeded to open the old metal trunk to retrieve some papers. He located them and gave to the SI for scrutiny.

The SI took his own time to go through those papers and was satisfied that they were genuine. His eyes fell on the three band radio on the table and demanded papers which were promptly produced. The license for the radio from the postal department was also produced for scrutiny. He handed them back and without a word went back to the jeep. Venkataswamy also followed and got in.

After the police jeep left, all the neighbors gathered in front of my grandpa's house and whispering the incident among themselves.

My grand pa was speechless and grand ma was sobbing inconsolably.

It was my grand pa's turn to recover console her as nothing untoward happened. Other females also joined in consoling her.

After this incident, my grand pas visited the market place many times and encountered his cousin sometimes but he gave Venkataswamy a wide berth whenever he came his way.

Tag words: Charge man, Foreman, police constable.

The Miracle of Dantilingi, Odisha

When Mother Mary defeated Yama raj, the Hindu God of death

Johnny Relevant, got a job as senior faculty in Diploma level engineering institution at Gopalpur, Odisha run by NTTF Bangalore; they run such industry compatible institutions all over the country. The courses are of more practical in nature than theory and so the placements are guaranteed every year as industry finds the students more practical oriented than bookish learning by rote.

JR found himself uprooted to a strange town but the job was interesting as he has to design practicals as per the syllabus. His goddess sent him there away from the defence industry of Hyderabad and the ever vigilant overzealous security apparatus.

It looked like his notoriety has preceded his arrival and he was welcomed with a reception fit for a head of a state. The attention lavished on him was both flattering and embarrassing. During his shopping in town, he was always followed by at least one armed cop in uniform and there might be many more in plain clothes ready to pounce on him given a slightest opportunity. Some cops actually pointed their fire arms at him and one SI touched his revolver holster when he casually glanced at him. JR was amused at all that attention but watched passively always remembering the commandment of the goddess "not to mock them"

During his interactions with the students, he came to know that many of them are children of illiterate tribal parents. He was pleasantly surprised to know that they have excellent reading and writing skills in English thanks to the dedicated service of missionaries. Right from pre- primary to high school they are taken care of by the missionaries and many of the alumni have risen to high levels even in private industry.

One of his students was by name Rajesh Behera, who is the son of Post master of a remote village called Dantilingi. His jurisdiction covers up to a small town called Soroda. The family of Behera are well off with 10 acres of agricultural land and are devout Catholics.

While exchanging his experiences and revelations of Mother Mary at Vailankanni, his student Rajesh Behera informed him that every year feast of Mother Mary takes place at Dantilingi on February 10. Hundred years ago when there was no transportation, French missionaries rode horseback in the deep jungles of Odisha and built a church for Mother Mary at Dantilingi. The legend of Mother Mary's appearance at that place and feast of February 10 every year was explained by Rajesh Behera.

It seems a century ago the village of Dantilingi and surrounding habitations were affected by an epidemic, about which he is not sure. It might be possibly cholera for which there was no effective cure at that time. People were dying like flies and one old lady appeared at the village and told the people to partake the water gushing from the spring on the nearby hillock.

The villagers rushed to the top of the hill which is about 300 feet high and sure enough, water was gushing from the crevices in the rocks of the hill. They collected the water and after drinking that it, the epidemic stopped. Rajesh said that as a proof of that miracle every year on February 10 as the prayer service starts, water comes out from the crevices of the rocks on the top of the hill. He invited JR to witness the phenomenon that year and JR was very much pleased with the invitation. He felt blessed to witness the miracle in person. He was told that the descendants of the missionaries attend the festival every year without fail.

So on February 8 he boarded the bus to Soroda, the nearest town along with Rajesh from where they have to find another bus.

They took a bus from Brahmapur to Soroda and there JR found a century old church and school run by missionaries. From Soroda they took another bus to Daringbadi also known as Kashmir of Odisha.

In one hour they reached the stop to Dantilingi and Behera's place is two kilometres from the main road. Behera senior, the postmaster came to pick him up on the motor bike and dropped him at his home cum post office. He made another trip to pick his son. After lunch the postmaster took him around to show the church and also the shrine on the hill top.

As the area is very remote, there is very less human habitation with small hamlets here and there. JR was surprised to find acres of irrigated agricultural land in the middle of the deep forest and wondered about the toll it might have taken on forest in clearing for agriculture.

Postmaster said" today this place is looking deserted with very few people but within three days you will see one lakh people will be gathered and you won't believe the crowd until you see it."

The next day the place was getting filled and the decorations at the shrine and the big church were in full swing.

JR was given a room for himself in the postmaster's residence and many of their acquaintances from nearby towns were also provided accommodation as there are no lodges in that small village. Even in Soroda eight kilometers, there are no lodges and so it was a great blessing to find room and bath in such a remote village.

In the night JR observed the police jeep making many rounds around the postmaster's residence and JR as usual ignored them. It seems Daringbadi is a hotbed of naxalites and B team was convinced JR has arrived to conduct secret meetings and chalk out some plans for executions.

On 10 February, the prayers began and as it continued, people rushed to the hilltop to get the holy water. Behera senior is a prominent member of the local church and instrumental in organizing the festival right from getting permission from the district police and myriad other issues.

After 10 in the morning it seems water came from the spring in the rocks and Behera senior handed him two spoonful of muddy water in a small plastic bottle. JR felt very happy and blessed to receive such a gift from heaven. He carefully kept the small cool drink bottle with two spoons of muddy water in his travel bag to carry it home.

He attended the church service and also carried the palanquin of Mother Mary in the evening. On 11th he took leave of The Beheras and returned to Brahmapur. He attended the college as usual and applied two days leave in the weekend to visit Hyderabad.

On reaching home, he reverently placed the small cool drink bottle containing two spoonful of the muddy holy water on the altar.

In those days he used to wake up at two o'clock in the night to light a candle for prayer.

As usual he got a candle and stuck a match to light it. Then his daughter Malathi sleeping in her room gave out a terrible scream.

He lighted the candle and rushed to her room to find the reason. He asked "Why did you scream in terror?

She said'1 saw a dark figure hovering over our apartment block"

They didn't give much thought to that vision and went back to sleep after prayer.

The next day around 10 in the morning, there was a commotion in the opposite flat and one lady was screaming in terror. The neighbors rushed to help her and were told that her husband locked himself in the bedroom after a quarrel.

It seems two brothers were sharing the apartment and the elder one got married seven years ago. He had a five years old girl child and later the younger brother got married and he was very devoted to the elder brother. His elder brother and his wife were like parents to the younger one and he could not think of leaving them to live separately. But the younger ones wife was pestering to leave them and threatening to commit suicide. He didn't bother but on that fateful day she threatened to file a dowry harassment case in the police station. The younger brother had enough and locked the bedroom from inside and hanged himself.

All the screaming of the wife brought the neighbors to the flat and some dynamic ones broke open the door only to find that person hanging from the ceiling fan.

The neighbors quickly brought the lifeless body down and rushed to the nearby hospital where they pronounced him dead on arrival.

Back to the home of Johnny Relevant: his daughter was utterly shocked and speechless. Then she said "Now I remember what I saw in the night. The dark figure I saw was a huge person with horns on his head and riding a huge bison. He threw a noose on our apartment building. But I know no one would believe me"

JR realized that A team headed by SN Yadav, the bete noir from his erstwhile job in HAL is alone capable of mounting such a spiritual attack. Many years ago he invited his daughter and her mother on the pretext of some female function and taken their photographs. With those photos he made dolls and placed them opposite each other so that there will be perpetual strife at JR's home. The end result he hoped that one of them would kill themselves to his utter satisfaction.

He also knows JR's place of work in the state of Odisha and his train trip to Hyderabad. He knew about his visit to his daughter and her mother. In this aspect, SN Yadav is better than B team who rely on technology to locate subjects with a circular error probability of two meters. But this demon SN Yadav successfully locates whereabouts of his victims with pinpoint accuracy. That is the power of witchcraft!

Next having got all the three together under one roof, he has to put the next part of the script into action; that is ignite a quarrel so that they kill themselves. However JR being aware of the schemes of that crook avoids all confrontations and not to play into the hands of that person. He is always very cautious as he knows about the schemes of that crook and swallows all insults hurled at him both his daughter and her mother without flaring up.

This SN Yadav managed to co-opt B team in his campaign of hate and they too tried their level best but could not kill anyone much to the disappointment SN Yadav. But invoking the God of Death to kill opponents is unheard of in the realms of tantra JR went on pondering about the possibility of using Hindu gods as hired killers to bump off innocents. Do they function as a hit men working for the highest bidders? He was much troubled by these thoughts ever since.

One good outcome of this episode is the blessing his daughter Malathi got by seeing Yama raj the Hindu God of Death, is long life. It seems whoever sees that God while living is blessed with long life.

JR went to Dantilingi next year also and some more times but the spring went dead in later years. He was convinced Mother Mary performed that miracle that year alone solely for him to display her power and love for him.

Hail Mary.

Tag words. NTTF Gopalpur, Soroda, Brahmapur, Dantilingi, Daringbadi, Mother Mary, Yam raj, the Hindu god of death, suicide by hanging.

Navanakki Nagappa

The faith healer of Gangavathi

The author while working in HAL was the subject of intense hatred with one worker from coastal Andhra making rounds of his quarters twice a day; once in the morning and again after work hours at night. In the morning he used to find coconuts and lemons smeared with vermilion in front of his quarter. There were no CCTVs in those days and one could not accuse anyone in the absence of any evidence.

One morning that worker sent his eldest daughter to my house to borrow one kg of sugar which is a normal practice among neighbors. But what perplexed me is the reason for him to borrow it from my house which is one km away from his quarter when all his co-workers are living next door. But without further thinking I measured out that sugar from my kitchen and gave her in a plastic bag.

After a week or so, same girl returned equal amount of sugar and I promptly added it to our stock in kitchen.

We started using that sugar and totally forgotten about it.

I started getting boils on my tongue and was unable to chew even bland food. My mouth was constantly on fire and I had to douse the fire with steady drinking of water. Then the inflammation spread to my throat and I used antacids tablets glucose for some relief.

The burning sensation advanced to my stomach and I was constantly feeling the fire in my stomach. I felt it is time to see the doctor.

I went to the company doctor and he recommended to visit a gastro entomologist. The specialist doctor at BBR hospital told me that there is growth of fungus in my stomach which was shocking. He prescribed some capsules costing 40 rupees each in those days. The dosage was three time a day.

After starting the treatment, the symptoms subsided and I was able to take normal diet. Once I stopped the treatment, the symptoms used to return. The doctor told me that there is no permanent cure to that condition and I have to take the medicines life long.

After leaving the job and loss of my factory, my financial condition worsened and I could not afford the treatment. I started to look for alternatives medicine but was not successful. There were no smart phones or internet in those days and so I had to rely on traditional sources. I contacted my childhood friend at Bellary and was told to meet one faith healer by name Navanakki Nagappa at Gangavathi, a small town in Karnataka state.

So I went to that town and was told that his house is very near to the bus stand. One rickshaw fellow took me to a old house nearby and I was told that the old man see patients after five in the evening. So we waited.

After five in the evening one old man with thick glasses came out and cleaned the threshold and the door with a broom. He sat on the raised platform and made the patient sit in front of him. Then he asks the patient to spread his hands palm down and stares intently into the eyes of the patient. Then he furiously does some calculations with his index finger on the floor shifting his gaze from the patients face to the calculations. The he pronounces his treatment.

My turn came and I sat in front of the old man. I too spread my hands palms down and looked at Nagappa, the faith healer. Behind those thick glasses his eyes looked enormous.

After doing furious calculations, he said I had to observe fast for 21 Mondays. The procedure is to eat to my heart's content up to 3'o clock in the afternoon of Monday and not to take even a drop of water till 6'o clock of Tuesday morning. He asked me whether I am willing to start that treatment and I answered yes. He tied a red tread around my right wrist and told me to go. No money was charged and he also did not enquire about my ailment.

I returned to Hyderabad and observed the fast for 21 Mondays with utmost discipline. The burning in the stomach went away and treatment was discontinued. The problem never returned to my astonishment.

That was long ago and I came to know he had passed away leaving no heir to that great tradition of mysterious faith healing.

Tag words; Gangavathi, Nagappa, fungal infection in stomach. Gastro entomologist, BBR hospital.

Ruknuddin Khalkamkhar

My spiritual father

My burning desire to become an engineer made me chuck my watchman job in railways and take a leap of faith into the unknown by joining an engineering college in Gulbarga. The salary was Rupees 330 per month with no allowances and no leaves. You get a fancy uniform with a four pointed two stars on the epaulets. It is strictly four pointed as per regulations and as some of the vainglorious SIPFs as they were called started wearing a five pointed stars, they were threatened with arrest by a railway police circle inspector for impersonating a police officer. That incident took out any glamour of wearing that uniform for me and it became very clear that force is only a watchman force with no real powers. And the promotions were very few as it usually takes ten years to get promoted that also on adhoc basis to be reverted back to the old post as the powers that be seem fit. All higher posts are filled by IPS or even state police inspectors to accommodate as comfort postings.

My younger brother was working and he promised to help me my college studies and so I joined that college. However within a month, he fell in love with a point's man's daughter and got married ending the promised support. So I slogged on and fell back on my father's earnings and after some months he also stopped sending any money.

I was evicted from the hostel for not paying the fees and took shelter in a friend's room. I used to walk two km for lunch in a dilapidated khanavali whenever I had money. For many days I had no money and was starving. Then one night I visited my friend Shariff's room and he gave me 10 rupees for supper. He promised that he will come to my room next day.

The next day he came to my room and gave 100 rupees to pay for a private mess. Food was taken care for one month.

I had another friend by name Pocheti Hanumanth Maruthi, whose father was a driver in the railways and used to pay him 600 rupees to him every month in those days when mess bill was around 200 rupees for a month. Unknown to his illiterate parents, he was failing in every semester and at the end of five years, he had a backlog of fifty papers including first semester English. I too tried to coach him in Basic English but could not make him learn anything.

He was from the railway quarters of Wadi station. After seeing my plight of destitution, he told me that he would take me to a holy man in his place. So I boarded a passenger train from Gulbarga and at Wadi Pocheti he took me to a small clinic run by Ruknuddin Khalkamkar.

He was around forty years of age and after Pocheti introduced me and narrated my situation, he told me take a chair. On a piece of paper, he wrote my father's name and my father's mother's name. A mysterious pattern was drawn on the paper and he folded it to make a talisman. He told me to keep the talisman sacred by not visiting a place where child birth has taken place and also places of bereavement. The he asked me to see him next day. I returned to Gulbarga to my college and went again as told by next day.

When I met him again, He said "your father has a heart of stone. Don't worry, I have taken care of him"

After reaching Gulbarga, I went to my bank to verify my bank balance. In those days there were no ATMs and one has to physically visit the banks for balance enquiry. The last time it was zero balance and I was surprised to find 150 rupees in my account.

Ruknuddin prayers made that stone hearted pitiless military grunt go to the bank and deposit that money in my account. Ruknuddin did not charge me any money.

That way the relationship grown with the saint and he helped me many times whenever I got stuck in a tight corner due to my follies only.

Then I completed my engineering and got a job in HAL. After the birth of my daughter, I was terrified of providing for her and used to take up works for DRDO contractors. For one private company I designed and made glove box controllers out of which one went to DMRL, one IISc, one to BHU and the last one I was not sure. After delivering the units, the contractor was dragging his feet in paying. There was no registration of my unit and I could not raise any bill to force him to pay.

Then another secret monk entered my life. It seems one monk used to visit my quarter and told my ex-wife about my pending payments. He advised her to visit my in-laws place and donate one sari to her brother's wives.

So I purchased sarees, went to Karnataka state and donated the sarees. After returning to Hyderabad, I got a phone call about the pending payment for which a check had been made ready.

I rushed and got the cheque and en cashed. Thus began my ordeal with the secret swami. He was running my life secretly by making many trips to Karnataka state without any rhyme or reason. That way my ex-wife made me lose huge amount of money not to speak of leaves. Even my daughter was made to lose attendance in school due to these trips to her native place, Unknown to me she was planning all the time to make me bankrupt by losing money and leaves by making me travel every week on some flimsy reason. I too was very naïve to fully trust her but she proved her predictions right the first five time but next hundred times she was playing a very destructive game in the name of the secret swamy.

Due to the effort of that invisible swamy, I got some property as inheritance. My mother promised the transfer in municipal records, but after taking money from me, she did nothing for several months. Then I had to go to that place and to my utter grief, my two younger brothers refused to sign the no objection papers. I was stuck with useless property which I could neither sell nor build anything on it. And I spent a fortune in getting my part in that property.

No trace of the invisible swamy as it seems he died of broken heart due to the scheming of my ungodly ex-wife.

It seems that monk told my ex-wife that he was going to bestow immense wealth on me but on only one condition; that is I should not marry anyone after receiving the blessing. Agreed to that condition as I was sick of that job. The procedure spelt was that after taking bath I must make a vow by touching Hanuman in one particular temple in Hospet.

It looked simple enough and I was over joyed for that simple solution to end my struggles. So I booked a train ticket and after taking a lodge and went to that temple the next morning. I touched that idol and repeated whatever was told to me. Then we returned to the room and came back to Hyderabad the next day. That was not the end as I thought.

After some days the criminal mind came up with another trick; it seems my vow was not in the right spirit and I had to repeat the whole exercise again.

So we all went and repeated the exercise and returned to Hyderabad.

Then after some days, she came up with another excuse; the second vow was also not in the right spirit and I have to repeat the process again.

We all went to the same temple, repeated and returned to Hyderabad. But some crooked plan was brewing in that criminal brain.

Suddenly she started accusing me of having an affair with a canteen waiter's daughter and the waiting wolves grabbed the golden chance.

Then the honey trap was threatening her to drag me to police station and get me beaten in lock up, on what grounds I could not think of. She was spreading calumny about me with the womenfolk in the township. There was no direct threat but only spreading lies and trying to provoke me to some sort of reaction.

After abandoned by that swamy I thought of my old guru and went to see him. To my great relief he was practicing in the same clinic and prayed for me and gave me a talisman. With that I went my native place and got some help from well-wishers who prevailed upon my brothers to sign the papers. My guru told me not to take any share from that property but donate to charity whatever I would receive. Many of my relatives had died in fights over that property and whenever I visited that place and slept there, my daughter would see many spirits running around that place in the night. But I could not do so as I was hard up for money and received whatever I could get in a distress sale.

Back in Hyderabad, the A team led by one SN Yadav, a proxy punching, free roaming, bootlegging pimp was working overtime to push their agenda in threatening with police action. My guru had ordered me not to speak to the honey trap as merely speaking to her will finish me off it and even God himself cannot save me. It seemed she was the devil incarnate but I had to bear all the insults silently she is spreading about me. Meanwhile regardless of any warnings, my ex-wife had a running battle with that honey trap. The battle was not between two women but I was the target and so watched with the sacred talisman always in my pocket.

My guru was a vegetarian and I was also not sure of his denomination whether he was a Sufi or Sunni, I was not sure. He used to advise me to pray to Hanuman ji and also told me to visit. There was a hand drawn figure on a card board sheet in his praying room and he permitted me to visit the inner sanctum sanctorum and pray to that image.

The much dreaded day had finally arrived and I was summoned to the police station. There the SHO gave me the choicest expletives and I silently heard it all. Then I was told give an undertaking in writing that I would not harass that "innocent "girl in future." Many workers also came to the police station in my support.

All the while the bitch who started it all ran away leaving me holding the can

Later when I met my guru, he said "you were in great danger in that police station."

Then started intense surveillance on the three of us I was much depressed after the much anticipated visit to the Balanagar police station. The expletives the SHO hurled at me made me realize that life is not worth living. The neem tree with low hanging branches was too tempting to attempt suicide. I was about to ignore my small daughter and planning my exit from this world. Again I visited my guru at Wadi and he said" Change your quarter immediately to a different line".

We were in quarter no C55 which was south facing in an east west row of quarters. So I applied for change of quarters in north south line facing east. I wrote to the admin office for change of quarter citing presence of snakes pit in the present quarters. As quarter no 95 was vacant, it was allotted and I started moving to that place.

But my ex-wife was adamant about not moving out and slept alone in that vacated Empty Quarter for another month not bothered about the child. I had to make her ready for school bringing breakfast from the hotel opposite the factory gate. Ruknuddin Khalkhamkar rescued us from suicide in that quarter no C55.

I got divorced but she would not leave me alone. I was visiting a marriage bureau after receiving a post card from them. There I was introduced to one rich innocent divorcee and I took her to meet my mom in Karnataka state. There she flared up for no reason and refused to meet my mom.

Anyway I was determined to marry her and fixed up a date for that occasion. Just three days before that 'marriage' Ruknuddin Khalkamkhar called me by phone that lady was not divorced nor had any property in her name. After the marriage her husband and also cops would come after me baying for my blood.

So I was saved in the nick of time or else myself with my daughter would have been on the roads. Later I saw her hobnobbing with some cops in uniform in a restaurant in Shankarmut. It seems she must have been on the payrolls of cops as an informer and working on the both sides of law. My guru saved me from a deadly gang in the nick of time. I owe my life to my guru.

Meanwhile the honey pot was back in the business of spreading calumny about me as usual. And she was bragging that she got me beaten black and blue in police lock up and I am shameless to continue to live even after that. She was spreading a rumor that I would come to the outer gate every day at 5 in the evening to see her on her return from work. Hundred people would gather at the gate to witness the spectacle and the entire township would be discussing it.

When I met him next time in Wadi, in my presence, he let out a roar on that honey trap.

Back in Hyderabad a politician by name Prakash goud came to know about her shenanigans in the township and called her father with a warning. It seems earlier she tried to play a gold digger with the politician's follower. Boosted with their invincibility in the factory premises, they played their hands and were cut to size by that Prakash goud.

The honey trap and her waiter dad shat in their pants, were terrified. Their braggadocio evaporated and they scampered away with their tails firmly stuck between their legs. She got married to one of their kind in a hurry ending her misadventure.

When surveillance intensified and vicelike grip of security agencies was tightening on me and family members, I visited my guruji once. There in my presence he heard a message from our goddess Huligamma; Which was "To donate a piece of cloth, a blouse or a sari along with home cooked food to any married lady on Fridays. To do this for about 11 weeks."

I was dumb stuck after this revelation and after reaching Hyderabad started performing this ritual. Some ladies accepted while others were suspicious as they thought we are performing some sort of black magic.

After 11 weeks an offer of voluntary retirement came from the head office in Bangalore which was exactly designed to my eligibility. I grabbed it and against strong opposition from our HOD, forwarded to Bangalore. My department tried their level best to stop me but me and our Goddess alone knew the danger we were in and I did not wish to become another Nambi Narayanan though I am not in his league. The media and the public would blow out any minor issue to an Oscar level ruining lives and reputations.

Many years later I visited Wadi railway station and was told that my guruji had left for his heavenly abode. His children disposed of their assets and relocated to Gulbarga.

None of his children were blessed to carry on his legacy which I found to be very painful. May God bless his soul in heaven.

Tag words: Wadi railway station, Quarters no C 55 &C 95 HAL Township, Ruknuddin Khalkhakar.

Cobra in a Catholic Church

Exorcism and a cryptic message

Johnny Relevant was unemployed for many years and was taking shelter in the place of is in- laws with his daughter at Hospet town. There while exploring about his daughter's education in a girls college he met a professor of Kannada. As he explained his situation, he became somewhat close to that professor who had wide ranging contacts in the field of education.

With his network both Johnny Relevant and his daughter got an offer as teachers in a residential school near Gangavathi in Karnataka state. He accepted that offer and left for that school which was located at a village called Saluvanchimara twenty kilometers from Gangavathi. Free accommodation was also assured for them near the school.

So he left his in-laws place with his daughter for that school and a lone building with only two portions was the official accommodation in which one part was occupied by the security in charge of the school with his wife. He was a permanent employee of that school. It was a lonely secluded place on the highway with labor quarters of the rice mill on the other side of the road.

They reached that place and unloaded their small luggage. After bath, JR started towards the school which was in the huge campus next to his quarters. As he was walking towards the school, a crow started chasing and attacked him. It went around and swooped down on him scratching his head. The omen seemed to be bad and he felt something was not right with that place. He returned to the room and took bath again before proceeding to the school and this time avoided the tree of the crow. Little did he know that they will be evicted mysteriously under the most humiliating circumstances after three months.

He was allotted intermediates math's classes for himself while his daughter was made teacher of primary classes. Lunch was provided in the school canteen while supper was made by them at the quarter. There was a village called Siddapur at a walking distance from the school where they used to buy provisions.

After some days his wife also joined them. Their first salary was paid on time which gave them some relief. Second month also passed with no incident. But in the third month a strange incident took place.

JR had to go to Hospet town on some errand leaving his daughter and her mother at that lonely place for one night. Around midnight a group claiming to be students returning from a sports meet started knocking on their door. JR's daughter were terrified but they did not open the door. After repeated banging they were shouting outside to open the door to get some drinking water. The commotion attracted the attention of the passersby on the highway and some of them reached their place to find out about the cause of the commotion.

Then the next door of the security person opened and his wife chided them for knocking on the wrong door. The "students" were reprimanded and told to go to the hostel for whatever they want.

When JR returned to the school next day, he was told about the incident in the night and he didn't give it much thought. It was the end of the third month of their work at that place. Next week all the staff were paid their salaries and told that they all are relieved of their jobs. That is they were all fired en masse.

Several months later a medium told him that the so called 'students' who knocked on the door of their quarters were coolies from the rice mill assigned to kidnap his daughter and bring her to the guest house. After that Giri had his way with her, she would be packed off to the harem in Bangalore and some wads of currency notes would be thrown at JR and his wife to keep their mouths shut. If they dared to go to police or courts, they would be permanently silenced by his henchmen. Such was the clout of that gang and no court would be able to do anything to that gang. That was what the medium told him.

JR and his family were stuck in that god forsaken place and didn't know what to do. He requested the chairman to allow them to stay for one more week to find alternate job and accommodation. It was accepted grudgingly and they hit the road looking for sustenance in that godforsaken place. Jobs are to come by with only the rice mills with starvation wages.

As they were told to vacate the rent free accommodation of the school, they found a nice home in upstairs of a rich businessman' house in the village at a monthly rent of Rs 2000/-

After being sacked again from another job at a nearby rice mill, he left that place unable to pay rent. They all found shelter in his in-laws home in Karnataka state leaving all their belongings in that rented place.

Between Sindhanur and Bellary, there is a village called Sirigere where a farmer donated one acre of his land for a church. The pastor running that was by name Francis. He was an employee of state electricity board a catholic by birth. Though married and having four children, he had an affair with his colleague's wife.

This preacher left his wife and children and was living with the other man's wife neglecting his family. He used to visit his home now and then to fight and beat his wife. During one quarrel he slapped his wife at which his mother also a devout catholic intervened on behalf of her daughter-in law. This Francis slapped his mother also. His mother cursed him to lose his hands.

Then Francis left his home in a huff on his Bullet Motorcycle and went to attend a break down call on a transformer. He climbed to the transformer and was suddenly electrocuted by the 11 kV power line. He fell down from the transformer and he was rushed to the hospital in Bellary was badly burnt in unconscious state.

JR took shelter in that church when they were homeless and hungry. One day while having lunch in the have food if no cook is available such people may cook their own food.

One day as they were having lunch after the prayers in the open place in the church compound, drops of red liquid fell on his daughter's dress from the sky. JR was shocked and looked around for any birds around and found none. There were no trees anywhere and wondered about the source of that liquid. It seems God, or Jesus foresaw some great calamity befalling on her and so shed his blood on her to shield her from the unforeseen calamity. Later it became clear that some invisible power protected her when she joined a college to pursue her education.

Her classes would start from 7.30 AM in the morning and to attend classes, she had to catch the first bus at 6; 30 in the morning. The bus stop used to be deserted at that time and unknown to JR, B team had opened a dossier on his daughter when he visited Balanagar police station on 11th September 1996. She was just five years old at that time.

It speaks volumes about the hard work and professionalism of Indian police to keep track of a child till she grows up and use their formidable resources and power to harass her. So from the nearby Pet Basheerabad police station they would drive up to the bus stop to heckle and discuss in front of her on how to kidnap and rape her. She didn't' know the purpose of this harassment and continued to attend the college. After college hours while returning by bus another bunch of thugs would follow her by jeep and harass her. This continued for some days, she was terrified and dropped out. When JR returned home to Hyderabad was told about the harassment of the law enforcement thugs fully confident she would not be able to identify them.

Then he recalled the incident of blood sprinkling from skies on her and prayed to the Holy Spirit of the promise of protection and waited. After some months four cops including an ASI were placed under suspension in a case of custodial torture. Then Mother Mary appeared to him in a church and told him to write about it in his Facebook account. That way B team got rewarded for their dedication to the duty of protecting the nation.

Le Culte naturel; dessiné et gravé par Mallet.

Now about A team's game plan of destruction.

One Friday, Francis announced that there will be baptizing in the church. In catholic tradition baptism is performed by sprinkling holy water on the subjects where as in other denominations, the subject is dipped in a pond or a small pool of water.

Anyway, after prayers were over, Francis sprinkled holy water on whoever is ready to get baptized. When JR' daughter's turn came the preacher stood in front of her and was unable to move. He glared at something in front of her and was warned by a dark entity not to come nearer. He gathered courage, sprinkled the holy water and she fell down unconscious. Nearby females caught hold of her and she slept in their laps.

After some time she woke up and told an extra ordinary account of the incident. When the preacher was coming nearer her, a huge dark snake came out of her almost standing as tall as herself warning Francis not to come near. He ignored the warning and sprinkled the holy water on her then the snake was burnt to ashes. There was a boil on her right heel where the reptile came out of her body. It took one month for the boil to heal completely.

They were all wondering on how anyone could manage to implant an evil spirit in a child's body and marveled at the power of holy water to burn it to ashes.

Then JR got a job somewhere and wanted to reclaim the abandoned belongings in Saluvanchimara village. It was more than 10 months since they left the village and the fate of their belongings was not known. If the owner demands full payment of pending arrears of rent it comes to around Rupees twenty thousand which was a huge amount. Yet he decided to meet the owner by coming from Hyderabad and visiting that village. Before going there, he wished to spend one night in that church of Francis. He attended the third Friday prayer and after every one left was sitting on a raised platform by the side of the church.

The church was deserted and JR was sitting alone and was shocked to see a huge cobra slowly passing by his side. He watched it silently and after going some distance away, it turned around and started watching him with its hood spread wide. Then it bowed its hood and went back the same way it came and JR could see it inside the burrow, He knew the cobra conveyed some message and he didn't know the content of that message.

He left the church and walked to the bus stop two kilometers away and caught a bus to Bellary from there to Hospet. There he had an old friend who works as a priest in a small temple near the foot of a neem tree.

He reached that place and spoke to the priest by name Narayana He explained the incident of the cobra in the church. Narayana closed his eyes for some time and finally opened and said" you are going to meet someone tomorrow. That person is going to bow his head to you and will be favorable to you."

Next day he left for that village where they had taken a house for rent and abandoned it for ten months. The owner had broken the lock and kept his belongings in a pile and gave the house for rent to someone else. The owner and daughter helped themselves to some sarees and pressure cooker also but agreed for payment of only two thousand rupees towards pending rent only.

He paid that money and gathered his belongings and reached Hyderabad after changing two buses. The message given by the cobra in the church manifested as prophesied by Narayana.

Tag word: Francis, Sirigere, Catholic Church, baptism, exorcism, Facebook.

www.ingramcontent.com/pod-product-compliance
Lightning Source LLC
Chambersburg PA
CBHW020325180726

47991CB00019B/706